THE CULT MOVEMENT

JOAN JOHNSON

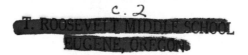

A GROLIER COMPANY

FRANKLIN WATTS I 1984
NEW YORK I LONDON I TORONTO I SYDNEY

Photographs courtesy of:

UPI: pp. 4, 21, 30, 38, 41, 45, 60, 83, 90;
AP/Wide World: pp. 24, 35.

Library of Congress Cataloging in Publication Data

Johnson, Joan (Joan J.)
The cult movement.
Bibliography: p.
Includes index.
Summary: Traces the history and analyzes the appeal
and the dangers of cults, or religious groups
requiring blind obedience to a living leader, which
have gradually grown in strength and popularity
during the past twenty-five years.
1. Cults—United States.   2. United States
—Religion. [1. Cults.   2. Religion]   I. Title.
BL2525.J64 1984   291'.0973   84-7417
ISBN 0-531-04767-9

CONTENTS

THE CULT
MOVEMENT

TO ROBERT H. SYKES
a teacher who really did alter lives

CHAPTER ONE

WHAT IS A CULT?

One day, you may open your front door to find two or three neatly dressed, smiling young people collecting for their church. They will be cheerful and friendly and, in return for your dollar, they might give you a bag of peanuts or some flowers. You might not be certain exactly which church you have just helped, but you will think, "What nice kids!" Or, you may be walking down the street in Boston or New York or San Francisco and stop to watch several strange-looking young men who have shaved their heads and who wear long, saffron-colored robes. They, too, will be collecting money or selling pamphlets about their religion, Hare Krishna. You may meet some friendly young people in a bus station or at a campus recreation center who seek you out and invite you to dinner. Or you may attend a meeting of people interested in bringing about world peace or developing a stronger personality and find yourself and your opinions the center of attention. Whether you know it or not, you have had your first contact with a cult.

Cults have been of growing concern in America over the past twenty-five years. People in the early 1960s brushed off cults as "just another fad" and paid them little attention. But in the last several years, America has realized that this "fad" is not following normal patterns. Instead of reaching a crest of popularity and then dying, cults have experienced steady growth. Even though some of the earlier cults are now no longer as appealing and strong as they were, others have formed to take their places. No accurate figures are available on the number of Americans who are now members of one or another cult, but guesses range from the hundreds of thousands to possibly as many as three million. Many cults have even larger followings outside of the United States. Not only has membership grown, but also the number of cults. Those who study the growth of cults estimate that at present at least one thousand of them exist in the United States.

Few people today are unaware of cults or shrug cults off as just another passing fad. They have heard something about cults on the radio or the TV or they have read something in the paper. Many actually know someone who has joined a cult or a neighbor whose child has joined a cult. Almost everyone has heard the name "Moonie" or the Unification Church or Scientology or Hare Krishna. Yet few are capable of defining exactly what a cult is and what makes a cult different from traditional religions such as Protestantism, Catholicism, and Judaism.

A religion is created when a group of people believe in a controlling, superhuman being or power who deserves their obedience and worship. The early Greeks believed in a whole system of gods and goddesses. Zeus was the most powerful of them all, but each god had special powers he or she could exert over men and women, and many had territories they ruled. Over the centuries as cultures grew, changed, or died, certain religions flourished. Most of these have been monotheistic— that is, their followers believe in *a single* God who has absolute power.

Although they believe in one God, not all have agreed on what that God is, how He should be worshiped, or what He demands of them. Consequently, new and different denominations, sects, or cults have been formed by people who disagree with others' beliefs. Sometimes an entirely new religion is formed. The early Christians, for instance, believed that Jesus of Nazareth was the Son of God, while Jews did not. Christianity became a new religion.

Different denominations are usually formed when people believe that certain laws, ceremonies, or rites should be changed. For example, the Puritans left England because they believed that God should be worshiped with stricter discipline than the Church of England required. In America, they set up their own colony and their own denomination or sect so that they could worship as they pleased.

Traditional religions and traditional denominations or sects are those groups that have been around for a long time and are commonly accepted by the society. New religions or new denominations are often called cults. A cult is a group of people who share the same religious beliefs and rites. By this definition, any religion or denomination could be called a cult. But in the last several years, the term *cult* has taken on new connotations in America. While the words *religion, denomination*, and *sect* seem to mean positive things, acceptable things, the word *cult* does not. Perhaps the reason for this is the cults' newness. Perhaps it is because new groups are often eyed suspiciously or not taken seriously. Perhaps it is because in the early years of any new group, its numbers are small or its lasting qualities untried. But the word *cult* now seems to imply negative things. Several events have occurred in the past two decades to cause this change in the word's meaning. One is the notoriety many cults have attained in the media. Their bad publicity, as we shall see in later chapters, has frequently been well deserved.

What then is the difference between traditional religions and denominations and the cults that have gained such popularity in the last few years? Not only are they new to us and as yet untried by time, they share other characteristics as well.

First, all have a living leader. The leader claims to have divine inspiration—that is, he claims that he has been chosen by God to receive and then communicate God's laws and

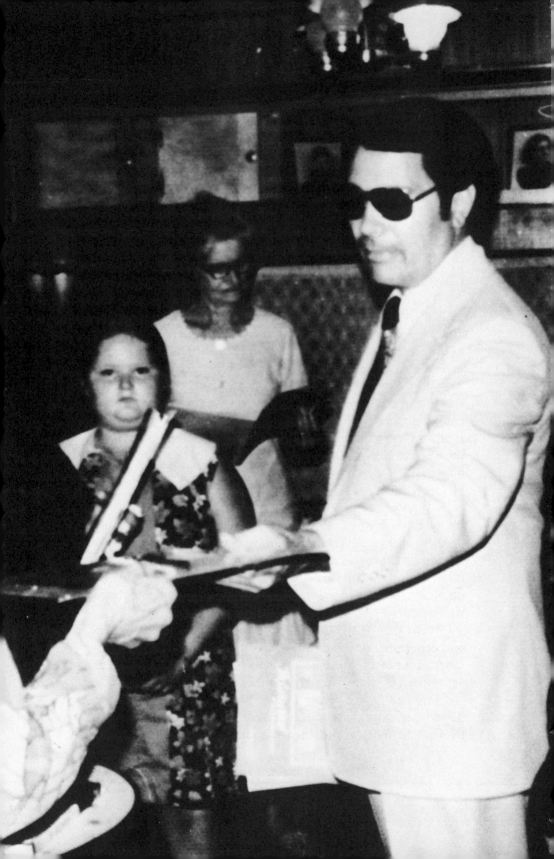

God's desires to the people. In a few cases, the leader claims to be more than just a medium through which God communicates. Jim Jones, the creator of the infamous Peoples Temple, at first claimed divine inspiration. As his power grew and his following increased, Jones began to believe he was God.

In 1978, plagued by scores of investigators and critics, Jones instructed the more than nine hundred members in his Peoples Temple Camp in Guyana to commit suicide. They did, although some had to be forced to drink the cyanide his aides administered. That his followers would obey him, even die for him, is the second characteristic of cults. The leader is the absolute judge of what is good and what is evil. He determines how his followers may live. He assesses the depth or sincerity of their faith. Because he is believed to be divinely inspired, he is not open to questions nor will he participate in reasonable debate. Anyone who challenges such a leader is thought to lack the essential faith necessary to be a true member of his church or cult. Like Jim Jones, most cult leaders require and get from their followers a blind obedience that can be used as the leader sees fit. If the leader is judicious, reasonable, and stable, that blind obedience can be used for good. If he is not, another Jim Jones and other senseless suicides easily could happen again.

It is also interesting to note that among the most powerful cults operating today, many leaders maintain luxurious lifestyles while their followers accept poverty as a voluntary sacrifice for their beliefs. Perhaps most noteworthy is Sun Myung Moon, whose luxurious estate stretches over many prime acres in New York State. His followers, on the other hand, live in group houses or communes and work most of their waking hours soliciting for the Unification Church or laboring without pay in one of the many Unification-owned businesses.

Jim Jones, founder of the Peoples Temple, is shown here wearing sunglasses.

The reward for their sacrifice, followers are told, is to be among God's chosen people. Most "Moonies," for instance, believe that Sun Myung Moon is the Lord of the Second Advent, that he has been chosen by God to change the course of the world by uniting all religions into one religion. They believe that he and Mrs. Moon are the Perfect Couple who will produce Perfect Children. They, too, can produce Perfect Children if their marriage is blessed by Moon. The forces for good are made up of Unification members who will eventually conquer all evil. Afterward mankind will live in harmony and God's favor.

Being among the chosen, then, means that the follower will be saved. Individuals who refuse to follow their leader's dictates will be among those doomed to damnation. Damnation in many cults is the same as damnation in many traditional religions. The soul will be the devil's property. The individual will be refused heaven's comfort and will reside eternally in hell.

The time of judgment in which those who follow are saved and those who refuse face God's wrath is, for some cults, an indefinite time in the future. Other cults, such as the Children of God, believe that the time of judgment is very close. It was the Children of God who in the seventies believed the comet Kahoutek would collide with Earth, beginning the final battle of the forces of good and evil. Armageddon is the name the Bible gives that battle. Armageddon will bring the defeat of evil. Armageddon will bring final judgment upon all sinners. The Children of God were so sure that Armageddon was about to happen, they poured out onto the streets to convince people to follow them and be saved. When Kahoutek missed Earth, they remained undaunted. Armageddon, they insisted, would happen later. The date was changed to 1993. And, they still maintain, only the most devout Children of God will be saved.

Cults use the idea of being among the chosen to exert pressure upon followers. It is easy to understand how faithful followers soon sense a superiority to all other people. In their minds, the others are not chosen. The others will not survive Judgment Day. The others are the devil's tools. Those who sacrifice and obediently follow their leader will be rewarded. Consequently, the faithful willingly tolerate poverty and endless work. Their blind obedience to their leader's rules seems worthwhile.

Unlike traditional religions, the primary goals of most cults seem only to be growth and wealth. Traditional religions can point to thousands of church-sponsored programs designed to help those in need in America as well as abroad. Similar programs sponsored by even the richest and most powerful cults are rare. While Jim Jones of the Peoples Temple was careful, frequently, to do a good deed for the benefit of someone he had heard or read was in need, he was also careful to alert the press, getting as much coverage as possible to further the Peoples Temple's public image. His charity was sporadic; his motives, obviously self-serving. Charitable programs are *not* priorities for most of the cults.

Not only are certain characteristics typical of the more well-known cults, but the effects they have upon their followers seem also to be similar. Because debate is discouraged and unquestioning obedience praised, followers learn to suppress critical thinking. They do not weigh, evaluate, or question the reliability of information they are given. They accept it, even if some of it makes little sense.

Learning to think critically is one of the most important skills an individual develops. How else can a person make wise decisions? In a world of the sincere and the insincere, of the believable and the absurd, individuals must make difficult decisions. Survival depends on the ability to think critically. That skill can be lost or its growth stunted if it is not constantly used. Imagine how differently history would have been written had Jim Jones's followers asked "Why?" If they had said, "Your reasons for drinking cyanide make no sense." But they didn't. They were victims of unquestioning obedience. They did not think critically. And now they are dead.

Although some cults stress the importance of the individual, most do not. According to Carroll Stoner and Jo Anne Parke, authors of *All God's Children*, the typical cult has little interest in developing a strong, adult personality in its followers. More often, group identity, as opposed to an individual identity, is the goal. The group is more important than the individual and individual needs are often ignored. In the Unification Church, many bright, creative "Moonies" spend their days collecting money door to door, a tedious task with few worthwhile challenges. In the Children of God, members have been instructed to use their bodies to entice members of the opposite sex to join or to buy their literature. The first demeans the strengths and talents of the follower. The second damages the recruit's self-image.

The longer a follower remains within a cult, the longer he or she allows the cult to override personal growth, the greater their dependency on the cult becomes. Some experts say that chances for a successful return to the world outside the cult can grow more slim as each month passes.

Many of these groups believe they have sole possession of true knowledge and are superior to the sinners who remain unsaved. They, therefore, are good; all others are evil. Good and evil become clear-cut. Unfortunately, in reality good and evil are not so easily distinguishable. If the thinking process which evaluates good and evil has not been used during the followers' stay with the cult, they find themselves incapable of thinking things through, of making decisions. When they leave, they are unsure of themselves, and rightly so. What has happened can be compared to a student who leaves piano class after two or three years of lessons. While classmates continue to practice and learn, the student merely listens to the radio. Then, years later, they are all put upon a stage and asked to play. While classmates play concertos, the student can only cope with five-finger exercises.

Consequently, the cult leader has free rein to decide what the followers will believe. Many leaders have abused their growing powers over the minds and spirits of their members more and more as members' critical powers diminished. Sidestepping the law is one example. Some cult leaders justify stealing if it is for the cause. Mail deception and misrepresentation while collecting door to door are two other examples. Some cults encourage bigotry and prejudice. Sun Myung Moon has been quoted as saying that Jews are responsible for the failure of Christ's mission and that the Holocaust, in which Hitler murdered millions of Jews, was a kind of atonement for their sins. Jim Jones influenced his followers to commit suicide and mass murder. The leader of Synanon, a famous organization for the rehabilitation of drug and alcoholic abusers, and two followers were involved in the attempted murder of an attorney who had won a court judgment against the cult. Members of other cults have testified of their willingness to murder for their leader and true faith, and former members of the Children of God live in fear of physical revenge or harassment for having defected.

There are other differences between the cults popular today and traditional religion. As we will see in later chapters, their methods of recruiting are often highly suspect and their manipulation of members questionable. They have become a powerful force in America today—a force that is growing stronger. Yet many experts believe that certain cults, which we will study, pose definite dangers not only to cult members but to society as well. The motives of some of the most well-known have often proved to be based not nearly so much on religion, God, and salvation as on greed, lust, and power.

CHAPTER
TWO

CULTS AND
THEIR LEADERS:
PART 1

Cults have always existed. Humanity's history is a patchwork of cults that, once created, have flourished, or died. At different times in our history, cults have taken hold more easily than at other times. Perhaps that is because people's needs change, sometimes requiring renewed interest in religion, sometimes replacing religion with other priorities.

Religious scholars see the 1960s and early 1970s in America as one of those times in which many men and women of all ages became more concerned with the existence of God. If their renewed interest was not in God in the traditional sense, they sought some knowable and attainable secret to the meaning of life. Some scholars call it the Third Great Awakening, seeing this as a time when humanity reassessed its role and importance in the universe and once again, through religion, sought some answers.

Suddenly new techniques for attaining those answers became popular. Transcendental meditation groups visited all but the most backwoods communities, offering peace and inner tranquillity for the price of a course. A formerly unheard of synthetic drug called LSD was tested by university professor Timothy Leary as a "mind expanding" method to pursue knowledge through uncharted passages of the brain. Zen, yoga, Tibetan Buddhism, ancient religions, rites, and philosophies, seemed to offer old answers to modern problems. All were characterized by a kind of internal seeking, implying that answers might lie within oneself, ready to be discovered.

Generally, the new movement discarded reason and logic as the proper tools for finding answers. Reason and logic, many felt, were limited. Together, reason and logic had been humanity's self-made, inefficient tools for understanding—and they had failed. They had prevented mankind from finding its answers. Traditional religions with their traditional interpretations and rituals were not necessary to find Him or Truth. God or Truth could be understood firsthand. Consequently, a chaos of strange new techniques from strange new schools of thought resulted. Someone "into" yoga one month might be taking courses in "primal screaming" or biofeedback the next. The selection seemed endless.

In the late 1960s, several events changed the direction these choices took. The gentle flower children of San Francisco's Haight-Ashbury, a famous "hippie" colony, had offered small bouquets and words of love and peace to strangers. But they had been replaced by or had turned into heavy drug users, drug dealers, prostitutes, and pimps. Charles Manson and his cult followers brutally and senselessly murdered famous actress Sharon Tate and her house guests. Chaos had indeed resulted from "do your own thing" and "find your own answers."

By the early 1970s, a new trend was obvious. It was still religious in nature, but its emphasis was different. "Doing one's own thing" created too many uncertainties. It did not appeal to those who wanted clearly defined and understood answers, nor to those who desired practical, prescribed ways to live their lives. The cults that became most appealing, then, were those that offered answers, and from answers, salvation. The Hare Krishnas, dressed in their identical robes, offered strict discipline, structured daily life, and ritual chanting as a means of attaining understanding and bliss. The Unification Church led by Sun Myung Moon looked forward to a time when all religions would be united into one—the Unification Church. The world would be ruled by a benevolent religious leader—presumably, Sun Myung Moon. All one had to do, their missionaries assured potential followers, was live by the rules Moon set forth in his *Divine Principle.* Because Unification centers often bought clothing by the truckload, Moonies tended to dress alike. Detractors said they looked less like converts than clones, but they were conventional, clean-cut, and wholesome-looking.

Cults in the last twenty-five years, then, have flourished in two different phases or time periods. They also share many other differences. Cults are, in fact, so diverse that generalizing is difficult. Consider numbers alone. Some cult watchers scoff at the conservative estimates of one thousand cults existing today, maintaining that five thousand would be closer. Some cults may only be known by their members. Followers may number only a handful or in the thousands. Some receive little or no notice from the press. Others, such as the Unification Church, may be under constant scrutiny. Some require secrecy; others promote their public image. It would be impossible as well as fruitless to try to cover them all.

Still, because they have so many traits in common, one can draw conclusions about them. Although little is known about the majority of cults, the most popular and powerful have been studied by religious researchers and the media. Books and articles have been written by ex-cultists, and many of the cults themselves publish an assortment of pamphlets and books to promote public understanding of their organizations.

Some of the cults we will mention are Americanized versions of Eastern religions. Hare Krishna, for instance, is a centuries-old religion that thrived in India long before America was even discovered. The Divine Light Mission, led by the

Maharaj Ji, is a splinter group that has been Americanized by its young leader, while his mother and brother continue its traditional philosophy and practices in India.

Other cults have their roots in Western religions, primarily Christianity. Some are extremely conservative, analyzing and interpreting the Bible on its most literal level. Others have begun as Christian movements but have moved away from those doctrines, often creating new "bibles" that have little connection with traditional Christianity. The most noteworthy of these cults is the Children of God, which has replaced old sacraments and sacred writings with founder David ("Moses") Berg's "Mo Letters." The Children of God movement has traveled so far afield that in an investigation by the attorney general of New York some letters were described as pornographic.

Another difference among cults is that while some began as religious movements, others became religious for the tax-exempt advantages the U.S. government affords religions. Additionally, the protection of religious beliefs and practices so carefully set down in our Constitution allows them to operate more freely. The religiosity of some cults, then, is doubtful, but they are included here because their techniques and goals are the same and their effects on "converts" similar.

Some of the cults that are described below are now thriving in the United States. Perhaps the richest and most powerful is the Unification Church. Scientology and Hare Krishna are also doing well. Other cults have peaked in membership and popularity and are now on their way out of favor. The Divine Light Mission, for instance, has sold many of its holdings in recent years. Synanon's yearly recruitment is a fraction of what it was. The Peoples Temple is now defunct. Yet it is one cult that must be discussed to fully understand cult personality and behavior. Nine hundred fourteen Peoples Temple members died by Jones's command. Jones died with them. Although the cult is dead, Jones must be studied, because for many, he is the ultimate symbol of the danger of cults.

Other differences are in cult recruitment strategies. Some cults are extremely aggressive in seeking out new converts. The Unification Church and Hare Krishna look for potential recruits on street corners, in airports and bus terminals, at campus centers, or in advertisements. Others depend on what they call the "witnessing," which their members do to persuade friends or fellow workers of the cult's benefits.

Cults also seek different kinds of recruits. Moonies, for instance, are usually young people aged eighteen to thirty. Scientologists are more likely to be in their mid-twenties. The Peoples Temple recruited both young and old. Many of those who died with Jim Jones were living on social security. Without question, however, the majority of cult recruits are in their late teens, their twenties, or their early thirties.

Some cults are communal—that is, once a recruit joins, he or she lives in a camp, on a ranch, or in an "ashram" with other cultists. Others bring followers together for meetings, but expect members to live independently. Some have members living both communally and independently.

Most of the cults have strictly prescribed rules and regulations. In the Unification Church, for example, great emphasis is placed on chastity. Meat, eggs, tobacco, and alcohol are prohibited in Hare Krishna. Some cults define sin as described in the Ten Commandments; others see only ignorance as sinful. At the other extreme, the Children of God has encouraged female prostitution as a means of acquiring recruits or power.

Cults also take different stands on the use of drugs and other chemical substances. The Love Israel family lost two members several years ago during a toluene-sniffing ceremony. Other cults are furiously opposed to drugs and are known to have helped users kick their addictions.

It is important to recognize that cults are not identical. They are as diverse as their numbers. On any issue, cults representing a spectrum of stands can be found. From Eastern to Western in their philosophies, from nonreligious to religiously conservative, from moral to amoral, from striving to defunct, each cult is different. Before turning to some of the most active cults today, we shall first look at those that have peaked in the last decade.

JIM JONES AND
THE PEOPLES TEMPLE

Jim Jones was a lonely boy from Lynn, Indiana. In 1964 he became a Disciples of Christ minister but later began his own sect. He found his followers among the poor, offering them dreams of racial equality, social justice, and inner peace. He also enchanted many well-educated, middle-class idealists who believed that Jones's aim was to build a better world. As a preacher, his beginnings were modest, at best. There was never enough money to do the things he wanted to do.

Eventually, Jones learned how to manipulate people and finances more efficiently. He accrued an income of $65,000 per week, some of it from followers' paychecks. Some of it was from the government—either signed-over social security checks or foster-care allowances for children of whom he and his administrators had been made guardians.

He had learned to control his people in other ways, too. For example, a common requisite for consideration as a loyal follower was a signed affidavit admitting some crime or sexual perversion. To prove their loyalty, followers signed these statements without realizing that later, should they give Jones any trouble whatsoever, those statements could be used against them. Jones used them frequently. A member who disputed him could easily be silenced and forced to obey. Should a follower desert the cult, perhaps reveal some of Jones's secrets to the media, Jones could easily discredit that testimony with the affidavit.

Jones thought nothing of breaking up families. Marriages were not sacred to him. He also found that having parents assign him their children's guardianship was a powerful tool to keep them in line. When it came time to move his followers to their new Guyana settlement, supposedly the Peoples Temple's "promised land," he had the power to send along whatever children he chose.

Guardianship of the children gave Jones other privileges as well. His sexual aberrations and the sexual abuse of the children in his care have been widely documented. According to Kenneth Wooden, author of *Children of Jonestown*, so perverse were the tales of child molestation, both in Guyana and back in California, that one Guyanan official refused to believe them. They were just too incredible.

Other forms of child abuse were the hard labor he forced them to do in building the Guyana settlement and the torture that ensued if a child failed to measure up. Some were punished by being dangled by a rope inside an old well. Inside, adults grabbed at their feet and made monster noises. According to Kenneth Wooden, others were given 100 to 200 whacks of 250-pound Ruby Carroll's "board of education."

How could such an obviously sick person continue to hold a following? Why didn't all of his people desert him? Certainly many must have known that Jones had gone beyond the realm of the sane, and that his actions were immoral, if not openly monstrous. Yet they stayed—and here lies the real danger of cults and their self-proclaimed leaders or messiahs. In the beginning, Jones's dreams were good dreams—an end to poverty, justice for all, peace, equality, and freedom. In the beginning, Jones offered hope. He did help many by supporting them, by building their morale, by helping them financially, and by being a friend. So good was he at convincing and converting that at one point his followers numbered twenty thousand. He convinced them that they could build a "new land," in Ukiah, California. There they worked together and worshiped together. The community was praised by those who visited, and grew powerful in Mendocino County. Later, he opened his Geary Street Temple in San Francisco, and his power grew even greater.

He preached socialism and took special pains to seek out the poor and the lonely. He practiced faith healing and the gullible believed he could cure cancer and help the lame to walk again. They believed they had seen miracles. Those who knew his tricks excused them, believing that the growth of the church was more important than honesty. At first he claimed to be the inheritor of the spirits of Jesus, Buddha, and God. In the last few years of his life, he believed he *was* God.

The Peoples Temple worked hard for public acceptance. A shrewd politician, Jones was careful to court newspapers, politicians, and other powerful personalities. He developed a reputation, Kenneth Wooden tells us in *The Children of Jonestown*, as "a humanitarian whose religious works were dedicated to helping the poor and uplifting society's failures."

Jones used his followers in many political campaigns to favor candidates who could later return favors to Jones. According to Mrs. Wayne Boynton, chairman of the Mendocino County Republican Party, as quoted in the *Los Angeles Times*:

> They were a dream come true. They would do precinct work. They would get information from the courthouse. They would do the grubbies—addressing envelopes, making phone calls. They'd do anything you'd ask, and so quickly you couldn't believe it.

Often followers worked all their waking hours doing menial jobs for a candidate. Their usefulness made Jones's support particularly appealing to politicians. Political indebtedness meant favors could be expected in return. Good publicity, help with some red tape that might be preventing Jones from getting something he wanted, lower-echelon government positions that could provide inside information before it became public could be expected from grateful winners. This was a part of Jones's master plan to grow more and more powerful.

Jones did his share. He was at one time or another foreman of the Mendocino County grand jury, had a seat on the County Juvenile Justice and Delinquency Prevention Board, and made sure he was photographed with or praised by such famous personalities as Governor Jerry Brown, Hubert Humphrey, Roy Wilkins, Jane Fonda, and Walter Mondale. Many celebrities came to speak at his Temple. Even Mrs. Jimmy Carter had a private dinner with him in 1976.

Jones was also careful to encourage good public relations. He chose a case for charity and then made sure the newspapers heard all about the Temple's good deed. In addition, he sent his followers off on bus trips from California to other parts of the United States. His followers gave bus-side shows, singing and telling of the beauty of their new religion. Few outsiders realized that these crowded, uncomfortable, exhausting trips with few rest stops and cans for toilets, were another means Jones had found to exploit his followers for his own purposes.

If Jones was sane at the outset of his ministry, something most certainly had happened to his stability by the end. A famous nineteenth-century psychologist and scholar, William James, might have the answer to what that something was. In *The Varieties of Religious Experience*, James explains that often the leaders of religious groups, those that have visions, have "a psychopathic temperament . . . [they] actually feel themselves played upon by powers beyond their will." If one believes that some super-power, God, is visiting him or her in visions, dreams, and frenzies, that one has somehow been chosen, it is only logical that the person also feels incapable of controlling that power. Since the person thinks there can be no control and that he or she can be tumbled about at the whim of that great force, instability results.

Another explanation was offered by Syracuse University anthropologist Agehananda Bharati. Jones might have reached what is called a "snapping point," a point of no return. The process begins with the sincere belief in one's divine calling. In order to lead effectively, the individual must manage his followers, keep them in line, and see to it that his power grows. Unfortunately, the quest for power eventually becomes more important than the quest to help humanity. In Jones's case, that most certainly happened. If anyone crossed him or if a follower complained or criticized, Jones attacked either with harassment, blackmail, or threats of violence. Women and boys were required to do his sexual bidding. Character campaigns were leveled against outsiders whose questioning became too perceptive.

Jones kept his followers in line through divide-and-conquer techniques. He used children to spy and tell on their parents, husbands on their wives, wives on the husbands, friends on their friends. No one could really trust anyone. If Jones heard of a complaint or a criticism, the offender was publicly degraded and punished. He often held all-night, emotional confrontation sessions in which followers were humiliated, denounced, or even beaten.

As his need for power mushroomed, so did his paranoia. He thought the world was against him. Anyone who criticized him was the devil's tool. Those who left or outsiders who criticized him or his cult's practices were threatened with death or injury or were made victims of malicious vandalism. As hints of something wrong within the cult became more and more widespread, the media and certain government officials launched investigations. According to *The Children of Jonestown*, he countered by creating a "Diversions Department." Critics were bombarded with letters and anonymous phone calls or accused of homosexuality or other deviations. This way, Jones diverted attention away from the Peoples Temple and put the investigator on the defensive. This also tended to dissuade others from looking too closely.

Eventually, as more of the truth about the Peoples Temple became known, Jones came to believe he was the target of a massive conspiracy. He convinced his followers that they, too, were in danger, and that their only protection and hope of salvation was through him. Jones now spent his energy on combating the enemy. He created what Konrad Lorenz in his book *On Aggression* called "militant enthusiasm by which any group defends its own social norms and rites against another group not possessing them." Followers were "ready to abandon all for the call." The Jonestown camp in Guyana became a kind of last stand. If governments could follow them there, prying, questioning, perhaps forbidding, then that is where they would make their last stand. And that, of course, is exactly what they did.

Jones dreaded an "exit" mentality—that is, he did not want to let anyone leave Guyana because he feared others would follow. According to Dale Parks, a nursing supervisor quoted in *The Children of Jonestown*:

> If a person wanted to leave Jonestown or if there was a breach of rules, one was taken to the extended-care unit. It was a rehabilitation place where one would be reintegrated back into the community. The people were given drugs to keep them under control.

Jones was also heavily into drugs. His physician, Dr. Carlton Goodlett, told Temple lawyer Charles Garry that "Jones is literally burning his brains out with drugs."

A custody battle with the parents of seven-year-old John Victor Stoen made matters worse and should have been an indication of how bad things were at Jonestown. The Stoens had left Jones's cult, but Jones had John Victor and would not release him. He claimed he was John Victor's sire and did not want him to leave Guyana. The courts in Guyana and California took his parents' side and demanded that Jones release the child. In *The Children of Jonestown*, Deborah Blakey, a former official of the Peoples Temple, reported that:

Jim Jones' Peoples Temple ended tragically when more than nine hundred of his followers committed suicide by drinking a cyanide-laced potion from this vat.

—20—

Terri J. Buford, public relations advisor to Rev. Jones, and myself were instructed to place a telephone call to a high-ranking Guyanese official who was visiting the U.S. and deliver the following threat. Unless the government of Guyana took immediate steps to stall the Guyanese court action regarding John Stoen's custody, the entire population of Jonestown would extinguish itself in a mass suicide by 5:30 P.M. that day.

According to Kenneth Wooden, Jones planned to burn the members of his church to death. In preparation, all babies "had been given small doses of sleeping pills that day so that it would be easier for them to die."

In November 1978, acting on numerous complaints about Jones and his policies, Congressman Leo Ryan brought an investigatory group to Guyana. Jones apparently felt that the end was near. He sent an execution team to kill Ryan and his group as they departed, while he readied the camp for mass suicide. The cultists had already rehearsed their death forty-two times in a drill called "White Night." They had developed a siege mentality. The drill had been effective. They were ready for their last stand. They drank the cyanide his administrators prepared. Some tried to escape, but most lined up docilely, drank the poison, and settled down in small groups or family units to await its effect.

Jones is an example of the cult leader, the messianic personality, gone haywire. He wanted the world to remember him. Over nine hundred people died. He left a bitterly ironic warning. Believing that he was a martyr for a world headed for destruction, he had a crude sign nailed above the platform from which he watched his people line up to die. It read: "Those who do not remember the past are condemned to repeat it." Jones might not have realized then the additional meaning that quotation took on when officials surveyed a camp strewn with over nine hundred bloated, decaying bodies. Certainly those who do not remember what a strong cult leader can do with submissive, unquestioning followers may live to see the same thing happen again.

DAVID BERG AND
THE CHILDREN OF GOD

The Children of God and David Berg are another example of a cult and its leader who, in his quest for power, begins to believe he is a messiah, someone expected to deliver his people into a promised land or a promised state of grace. Berg began as a Baptist minister in a small church in Valley Farms, Arizona. When he was dismissed, he traveled to California and worked for a television evangelist named Fred Jordan, preached in a teen coffee house, and began a movement called Teens for Christ. His following grew and eventually their name was changed to Revolutionaries for Christ and finally, the Children of God.

Part of Berg's appeal to young males was that he could ordain them as ministers, thus exempting them from the draft and keeping them out of Vietnam. Fred Jordan allowed him TV time, enabling him to solicit funds over the air and gain legitimacy through strong public relations. The Children of God cult grew quickly and by 1974 an estimated 120 communes existed in the United States.

Although at the beginning of his preaching career, Berg's view of God, morality, and devotion were in line with his Baptist beginnings, by the late sixties he was preaching a new gospel—according to "Mo." He had renamed himself Moses Berg, perhaps seeing a connection with the biblical Moses who led the Israelites out of Egypt to the Promised Land. He began writing letters to his followers and letters to the public. These were sacred to his followers, replacing study of the Bible. Berg told them that he was having regular revelations from God. He believed he had become a super-power, capable of knowing the future and of withstanding all opposing forces. "You could

even rebuke the devil in the name of David and he will flee. No power in the world can stand against the power of David," Berg said.

It wasn't a church he had started; he had no churches. But having been blessed in his mother's womb, he said, he was now truly a visionary and his letters would be used to communicate these visions. The Bible, although suitable for yesterday, was not in touch with today. His "Mo" letters were the word for today.

Children of God recruited aggressively. At its peak, it numbered approximately five thousand followers. At one time, Berg believed that the end of the world would occur with an earthquake in California. On the street, his followers warned people that Doomsday was impending and that they must join the Children of God before the Judgment Day. Later, he prophesied the comet Kohoutek as the Final Hour. Berg was wrong both times, but that didn't stop him. He changed the dates, deciding that 1986 will be the beginning of the end. According to Berg, Israel will be invaded by Russia. Israel and its ally, the United States, will be defeated. For seven years, Communists will rule the world. Then in 1993 the world as we know it will end. Only those most loyal Children of God will be saved.

Loyal Children of God must spend their time recruiting and collecting money. Like Jones's followers, they sign over to Berg all worldly possessions and learn ways to manipulate parents to get more money, if there is any in the family. They fill out extensive financial forms, listing trusts or any other possible sources of revenue, so that no potential wealth is left untapped. According to researchers Carroll Stoner and Jo Anne Parke in *All God's Children*, having once assigned their world-

Barefoot members of Children of God march along a busy street in Miami, Florida.

ly wealth to Berg, all but the highest administrators live in poverty. Berg and his top men live in the luxury their followers' wealth allows them.

Attorney General Louis Lefkowitz of New York, who conducted an extensive investigation of Children of God's operations in 1973 and 1974, said Berg takes "a positive position" on such things as incest and intercourse at a very young age and does not revere such institutions as marriage and the family. In other words, Berg encourages all manner of sexual immorality and does not believe in the sacredness of marriage. In one letter called "The Look of Love," Berg tells his recruiters: "If there's real spiritual contact in a look, it's just like getting naked into bed with someone." Lefkowitz found, among other things, that Berg advocated prostitution for his female missionaries. Testimony from ex-cultists is even more damning. According to the Lefkowitz report, a fourteen-year-old girl said that after having complained about being repeatedly raped at one COG commune, her leader told her that forced sex would "increase the tribe." According to a *Newsweek* interview with Herbert Wallenstein, who helped head the investigation for the state of New York, Berg's scriptures are "blatantly pornographic, complete with sketches and diagrams. We didn't even want to reproduce them in our report."

Under pressure to appear in a countersuit for disclosure of funds in 1972, Berg shipped most of his followers to Europe. There, many of his American recruits head his missions. According to Stoner and Parke, Berg was last reported living near Florence, Italy. But the Children of God cult is not dead. Many members, say Stoner and Parke, are still quietly recruiting in America. Others are operating under several aliases— Contact Jesus, the Christian Faith Association, and Toronto Christian Trust Ministry are three.

Although operations in the United States have been toned down, the Children of God still represents several threats. Many parents of recruits haven't heard from their children in years, have no idea where they are, or even if they are alive.

And the Children of God, still maintaining ties in the United States, could return at any time if conditions warrant it.

CHUCK DEDERICH
AND SYNANON

Chuck Dederich did wonders with the dregs of society, people who, unable to cope, had turned to drugs, alcohol, or crime. Synanon was founded by Dederich in a store front in Santa Monica. It grew wealthy and powerful, boasting two thousand members, and eventually took up residence in West Marin, California, in 1964. There some nine hundred people lived communally. Synanon offered an alternative life-style that turned many people's lives around, giving them a purpose, helping them to fit in and become happier human beings.

Synanon's early publicity was overwhelmingly positive. Dederich appealed to America's belief in a "down to earth" leader who could talk sense into the heads of his followers. It didn't matter to anyone that at that time (September 1976 to September 1977) he was drawing an annual salary of over $75,000; his son Charles, $30,000; Cecilia Dederich, $15,000; and William Dederich, $50,000; or that he had been granted a $500,000 retirement bonus.

According to Mitchel, Mitchell and Ofshe in *The Light on Synanon*, so positive was Synanon's public image that the first Marin County grand jury that visited Synanon in 1976 criticized the county probation department for failing to send juvenile delinquents to Synanon for rehabilitation. Then a *Time* article published in 1977 claimed that Synanon had turned into a "kooky cult." In 1978, another grand jury found serious flaws in Synanon's organization. Synanon had experienced a high number of runaways. Many claimed that they had been abused. Others reported possession of weapons, fears of landholders near Synanon's borders, and manipulation of those within its borders, all causing concern in Marin County.

Dederich's leadership closely follows the pattern of Jim Jones. Dederich underwent a change in the quality of his leadership from good works to power quests and paranoia. In the early 1970s, Dederich gave up smoking. So must everyone else, he declared. He shaved his head; his followers did, too. When his first wife, Betty, began dieting, so did everyone else. When Dederich decided whittling for thirty minutes a day was beneficial, everyone whittled. He decided that children were an indulgence, and within one week two hundred men had vasectomies. He conceived of a new marriage contract—a three-year, renewable agreement—and marriages ceased. When his wife died, he took applications for a new mate. About that time, he commanded a massive divorce and, according to Steve Allen in *Beloved Son*, 230 couples complied.

As the media got wind of abuses within Synanon, Dederich reacted with lawsuits. The *San Francisco Examiner* was sued for libel by Synanon and settled for $600,000. According to *The Light on Synanon,* serious probing of Synanon's operations was constantly hindered by the media's fears as well as individual fears of losing everything to Synanon's battery of lawyers.

Although at the beginning, Synanon preached healing, love, and nonviolence, it became an armed camp. Dederich formed the Imperial Marines, a group trained in the martial arts. The Imperial Marines were supposedly Dederich's bodyguards and protectors of Synanon's physical borders. Protect they did. When one "splitee," someone who had left Synanon, returned with his new wife in March 1978, he was reportedly beaten by the guards. They suspected he was a spy for *Time*.

Dederich said, "I'm quite willing to break some lawyer's legs, and next break his wife's legs and threaten to cut their child's arm off." He obviously meant it. By 1978, the Imperial Marines were taking their job very seriously. Phil Ritter, who was fighting Synanon in court to regain custody of his child, was clubbed and beaten by several unidentified assailants. In October 1978, Paul Morantz, an attorney who had just won a

$300,000 default judgment against Synanon, unwittingly reached his hand into his mailbox. The fangs that embedded themselves in his flesh belonged to a 4½ foot diamondback rattler whose warning rattles had been cut off. The snake had not climbed into the box. It had been placed there by two men who had been spotted by Morantz's neighbors. Joseph Musico and Lance Kenton, son of bandleader Stan Kenton, were charged with the crime. They pleaded *nolo contendere* (no contest) to conspiracy charges and were sentenced to a year in the county jail. Miraculously, Morantz survived.

Dederich was arrested in Arizona for conspiracy to commit murder and solicitation of murder. When he was found, the great reformed drinker who had developed a cure for alcoholism was so drunk he had to be carried out on a stretcher. He also entered a plea of *nolo contendere* to the conspiracy charges. He was ordered to undergo hospital treatment, was fined $5,000, and was placed on five years' probation. Recent reports say he lives as a recluse in failing health in Synanon's Badger Commune, a remote retreat that housed many of Synanon's leaders in the late 1970s.

Synanon didn't start as a cult. Its intent was not originally religious, but it did use those laws which protect religion for its benefit. In 1974, a letter from Dederich's lawyer suggested:

> If we are a religious community, and we are in the process of living our religion as a life-style, then state and federal constitutional guarantees of freedom of religion would offer complete protection against such legislative or bureaucratic interference . . . also . . . considerable advantage from a tax standpoint.

In other words, Synanon may have become a religious cult for practical reasons. It does share characteristics, however, with the cults in this chapter. The living is communal, the leadership, totalitarian. Followers contribute their personal wealth to its accounts, live by the rules imposed by its leaders, and finally, are fiercely loyal to Dederich. Dederich had said that "new-

Synanon's leader, Chuck Dederich, leaves the California court where he was placed on probation in 1980.

comers could be easily used to do the dirty work, scrubbing the floors, schlepping the pots . . . The good ones [newcomers] we keep, the rest we throw back." If a newcomer refused any order, he would be thrown out. So powerful was this "either/ or" threat that one member quoted in *The Light on Synanon* suggested that the next order could just as well be: "To stay in Synanon everybody has to go out and kill a gook or something."

By 1980, membership in Synanon was less than eight hundred, but Synanon's wealth has continued to grow. Synanon spokesmen maintain that the case against Kenton and Dederich was "trumped up." The cult still exists, although its rate of joining, over one thousand a year in the early days, has fallen dramatically. According to Steve Allen, spokesmen declare that Synanon's present goals arc "to continue helping people, to continue changing the world."

CHAPTER
THREE

CULTS AND
THEIR LEADERS:
PART II

While the cults discussed in Chapter Two might be considered dead or in a state of decline, the cults that are considered in this chapter are not. Perhaps the most noteworthy, a cult that will be especially emphasized in later chapters on recruiting and mind control, is the Unification Church led by Sun Myung Moon. Entire books have been devoted to this one cult, books that detail its complexity and delve into the many accusations that have been leveled against it.

LAFAYETTE RONALD HUBBARD
AND THE
CHURCH OF SCIENTOLOGY

Scientology did not begin as a religion. Ronald Hubbard founded it in 1951 with the publication of his book, *Dianetics: The Modern Science of Mental Health*, which was a national bestseller. Hubbard was a popular sci-fi writer at the time. He conceived of and designed the E-meter, which he later patented. The mechanism is a primitive lie and emotion detector. Subjects hold a tin can in each hand while they are questioned about painful or embarrassing experiences. A meter attached to the cans records the emotional stress resulting from each question. This process is called "locating engrams," emotional scars that have occurred either in the subject's present lifetime, the fetal stage, or in his previous lifetimes. Locating engrams is the first stage in liberating the soul. Engrams must be confronted and "erased" before the subject can become "clear" and operate to potential.

The system of "processing," in which the convert attempts to erase his or her engrams, is one of discussion and conditioning. The subject relives the bad experiences and faces up to them. This is done with the help of an "auditor," someone skilled in reading the E-meter and in discussion and confrontation techniques. Scientologists believe that if the convert can erase all engrams, he or she can achieve happiness in this life and freedom from death of the soul.

Scientologists do not remove themselves from the outside world. Their goal is to function within it effectively. To do this, they take courses. United States government attorneys investigating Hubbard believe that perhaps as many as a million people have been "audited"—paying for this service as much as $300 per hour. *Time* magazine claims that Hubbard's followers have paid up to $40,000 each for his courses and auditing sessions and that some individuals have spent hundreds of thousands of dollars in all. In its best year, Scientology's income was estimated at $100 million worldwide. Its membership may have been as high as two million worldwide. That estimate does not include people who took courses without actually joining the movement.

Although Scientology began as a "science," a kind of psychology, its leaders quickly recognized the benefits of religious status. In 1955, the group incorporated as a religion to "act as a parent church for the religious faith known as 'Scientology' and to act as a church for the religious worship of that faith." Hubbard, until recently, was head of the church and leader of the many auditors and processors who became its ministers. Meeting sites are called churches, and ministers perform marriages and baptisms. According to the U.S. Court of Claims in 1969, the beliefs of the church "center around the spirit or 'thetan' which is said to reside within the physical body of every human being. Scientologists believe that the spirit is immortal and that it receives a new body upon the death of the body in which it resides."

The January 31, 1983, issue of *Time* magazine says that Hubbard hasn't been seen for two years by most of his closest associates. No one is sure why. Some think he's in voluntary seclusion, which is what his top administrators maintain. His estranged son, Ron DeWolf, thinks he may have become mentally incompetent. Others think he is being held captive. Some even wonder if he's still alive. A judge however has dismissed the claim that Hubbard was dead or mentally incompetent on the basis of a declaration apparently signed by Ron Hubbard himself.

If what Hubbard claims about himself is true, his soul is alive. Having been reincarnated many times, he is already 74 trillion years old. He suffers, however, from many ailments and lives on vitamin injections and drugs. He's terrified of germs, says *Time.* He's also a recluse.

It's difficult to say very much at all with certainty about Ron Hubbard. Recent allegations by a man in possession of over five thousand Scientology documents Hubbard gave him for his biography have tended to discredit the background Hubbard would have the world believe. Hubbard gave them to his would-be biographer, Gerry Armstrong, when Armstrong was a member of the Church of Scientology, apparently assuming Armstrong would handle the information discreetly. Armstrong has since left the movement in disgust.

While Hubbard claims to be highly educated, Armstrong says he spent only two years in the engineering school at George Washington University before flunking out. Hubbard claims he fought in World War II and came home a hero after having sustained "nearly fatal combat wounds." Armstrong

The reclusive Ron Hubbard, founder of the Church of Scientology.

says he was given Navy disability for arthritis, bursitis, and conjunctivitis, none the result of combat. Hubbard was never near the front. Hubbard told his followers that between the years 1925 and 1929, he traveled through the South Pacific and Asia to absorb the "secrets of life" from holy men and magicians. Armstrong claims that, at that time, Hubbard was in high school—and not a very good student at that.

The Church of Scientology is trying to recover the papers Armstrong was given, but Armstrong is not the cult's only opponent. Ron DeWolf, Hubbard's estranged son, claims he used "criminal means" in his quest for fame, power, and money. Some ex-Scientologists claim that, like Jim Jones, Hubbard often had members confess in writing to wrongdoing and used the documents later to silence through blackmail. Several government agencies, among them the IRS, are also creating problems for Hubbard's operations that may require even further investigation into the organization.

In *Beloved Son*, Steve Allen states that the Church of Scientology has often been singled out as especially dangerous. He has heard again and again that one should "look out for the Scientologists. If they perceive you as an enemy, they can really come down hard on you." Many years ago, Hubbard developed a system of secret police, financial police, and watchers of the secret police. If followers got out of line, *Time* says, they were sent "to church prisons for rehabilitation." He did not stop, however, with internal control. In "Operation Snow White," he and his wife managed a system of spying that included five thousand "covert agents placed in government offices, foreign embassies and consulates as well as private organizations critical of Scientology." This network helped gather information on church opponents. Hubbard is said to have assembled files on many U.S. senators as well as on ex-President Nixon and the Rockefeller family; he also has a list of 136 government agencies in the United States and abroad that for any number of reasons have become "enemies."

"Snow White" resulted in a four-year prison term for his wife, Mary Sue, one of eleven members convicted of conspiracy to obstruct justice by covering up Scientology break-ins at Federal offices. According to Mary Sue, Hubbard writes her regularly.

At present, Scientology is faced with at least twenty-two civil suits, complaints ranging from charges of swindling to kidnapping. One lawyer, Michael Flynn of Boston, is representing twenty-eight people who charge they have been victimized by the Church of Scientology. Flynn says that he has been harassed by the church to the point that he now keeps a gun in his desk and, sometimes, bodyguards at his side. "I nearly died a couple of years ago when the engine of my plane quit. Someone had put gallons of water in the gas tank, but I can't prove who did it." According to *Time*, Flynn appears at the top of Scientology's enemies list.

Hubbard's son, Ron DeWolf, wants the court to protect his father's estate from Scientology's top administrators. They claim they are acting on behalf of Hubbard in trying to gain control of the more than $280 million in church assets. Others think that Hubbard is using the whole thing as a ploy to separate himself from Scientology's legal problems while still controlling the money. The IRS, meanwhile, wants $6 million in back taxes and penalties for the years 1970–1974. Investigators claim that certain income was not used for religious purposes. Should the IRS win, Scientology's problems may not be over. The IRS, according to *Time*, may begin looking into the records of other years.

GURU MAHARAJ JI AND THE DIVINE LIGHT MISSION

Guru Maharaj Ji was thirteen years old when, in the 1960s he was brought to the United States. His guru father had begun the Divine Light Mission in India in the 1920s. Maharaj Ji was

Guru Maharaj Ji greets three thousand young followers, many of them Americans, who traveled to India for a two-week gathering.

the product of a public relations campaign that quickly made him famous. At the height of his popularity he led an estimated fifty thousand followers in the United States and an additional twenty thousand in Europe and Africa. He came at a time when Eastern religions were popular. Americans were looking to ancient religions for what they felt was missing in traditional Western ones. He married at the age of sixteen, choosing as his wife a former airline stewardess. His mother, who continued to lead the Divine Light Mission in North India and Pakistan with the help of his brother, neither approved of his marriage nor the luxurious life-style he had begun leading. She disowned him. A power struggle between them over leadership was eventually settled out of court with a compromise. Maharaj Ji would lead the U.S. Divine Light Mission while his mother and brother would operate independently in India.

The Divine Light Mission, like Synanon, began by recruiting those living on the margins of society—the addicts, the lost. It promised that through proper meditation techniques, followers could make contact with God. DLM followers believe that God resides in the heart and making contact means the follower has achieved oneness with the universe.

Eventually recruits, called "premies," tended to be more conventional citizens—secretaries, administrators, and students. Their "tithes," a proportion of their income donated to the church, do much to support the Mission and the ashrams in which followers are encouraged to live communally. Because followers were more frequently solid members of the community, the personal incomes of the average "premie" increased, and so did the tithes.

Divine Light Mission recruits primarily through the "personal witnessing" done by its members. In that most "premies" work in the outside world, they have constant contact with others looking for something that will make their lives better. Followers are quick to explain the benefits of meditation and membership in the Mission. Divine Light has also advertised, pointing out the "spiritual highs" that can be achieved through meditation, which alters consciousness and supposedly expands the mind.

Spokesmen for the Divine Light Mission maintain that it is not a religion. Their guru sees himself as a trainer of meditation and self-discipline, including celibacy and abstention from drugs, tobacco, and meat.

Like the Hare Krishnas, Divine Light believes that evil or sin is created out of the ignorance of the mind. Jesus, an incarnation of God, tried to lead his people from ignorance and redeem them from sin. Maharaj Ji is also an incarnation of God in that he is trying to do the same thing. He is the second coming of Christ, the "perfect master for today." According to Joel MacCollam in *Carnival of Souls*, the guru claims he is a messiah, part of a line of Perfect Masters which in addition to Jesus included Buddha, Muhammad, Lord Krishna, and Shri Hans, Maharaj Ji's father.

At the height of its popularity, the Divine Light Mission's annual income was approximately $3 million. A good part of that supported Maharaj Ji, who enjoyed a luxurious life. The cult's overspending possibly required the eventual closing of several ashrams, which in turn meant less money for the central administration. The Mission has also sold some of its properties.

SWAMI PRABHUPADA AND THE HARE KRISHNAS

Swami Prabhupada was born in 1896. He died in the late seventies. He was educated at the University of Calcutta where he studied philosophy, English, and economics. He was a successful businessman, husband, and father before giving up his worldly life to become a Hindu monk. At fifty-eight, he left his home and family, first to become a meditating hermit and then, by Hindu stipulation, a homeless, penniless wanderer. He came to America at the age of sixty-one and, in 1966,

Krishna followers dance and chant
in downtown Minneapolis.

founded in Manhattan the International Society for Krishna Consciousness.

His cult drew many famous people, among them Alan Ginsberg, the poet. It attracted attention. No wonder. Devotees swirl and chant in their long robes. Men shave their heads to renounce pride, and women pull their hair back to renounce vanity. They stand out wherever they push their pamphlets and collect money, although recently some Krishnas have been dressing more conventionally for this work. They tend to be aggressive, and numerous complaints have been lodged against them for the zealousness with which they recruit and sell.

Krishna is not a new religion. It is an Eastern religion that dates back to 1486. It has no known founder. Krishnas believe in several gods—Brahma, the creator; Vishnu, the preserver; and Shiva, the destroyer. The second, Vishnu, has been reincarnated nine times. The eighth incarnation was Lord Krishna, the ninth, Buddha. Love for Lord Krishna is accomplished by dancing, singing, and chanting. The well-known chant— "Hare Krishna, Hare Krishna, Hare, Hare"—is used not only among Krishnas but in other Hindu religions as well. *Hare* means "the energy of God." The ritual singing, chanting, and dancing is a technique used to rid the soul of ignorance.

While Christianity teaches mankind's inborn, natural tendency to sin, Krishna believes that sin is caused by ignorance. In Christianity, salvation requires God's power, a force outside the self. Krishna salvation comes from looking inside the self and worshiping Lord Krishna. All material things have no importance. Luxurious belongings are rejected.

Krishna followers live a hard life, an ascetic's life. Celibacy is stressed and men and women are often segregated. Women in Krishna soon learn that they are inferior to men and that they need men for protection. Marriage is not encouraged, but permission will be granted if it is asked. If a couple conceives a child without permission of their swami, they may be "punished" by the birth of a girl. As inferiors, girls will have less education than boys in a Krishna school.

The cult is wealthy. Its members number in the several thousands. Sales of Krishna literature, buttons, and flowers support the organization. They also have an incense business, Spiritual Skies, which was last reported to net them over $2 million per year.

SUN MYUNG MOON AND
THE UNIFICATION CHURCH

Sun Myung Moon was born in 1920 to Presbyterian parents. He attended high school in Seoul, Korea, and studied engineering in Japan. He claims that at sixteen he had a vision in which Christ told him he was a messiah. By the time he was in his mid-twenties, he had already established a Korean following.

The present Unification Church was founded in 1951. It is based on a theology some scholars say he adopted from Paik Moon Kim, another self-proclaimed Korean messiah with whom Moon spent six months. The goal of the Unification Church is religious theocracy—that is, worldwide unification of all religions into one supreme religion that rules the world.

Unification philosophy is contained in their Divine Principle, a blend of Buddhism, Taoism, and Christianity. According to Divine Principle, mankind can be restored to God's grace with the coming of a new messiah and penance for sins. Restoration to grace will occur in several stages. The failed mission of Jesus was one. Jesus was to have married and begun a "perfect family," but he was crucified before he could accomplish the task. The Lord of the Second Advent will carry out what Jesus could not and will give man the opportunity to regain grace. Widely scattered implications in Moon's writing and speeches hint that Moon is the new messiah.

In a pamphlet cited by Carroll Stoner and Jo Anne Parke in *All God's Children*, that implication is clear. After mentioning the "universal significance" of Bethlehem on the night

Jesus Christ was born, the writer turns immediately to January 6, 1920, on which "an event of similar significance" occurred. It was the birth night of someone chosen to complete the "remaking of the world." Moon's birthday began the "Cosmic transition."

In the July 1983 issue of the *New Republic*, Moon is quoted to have said, under oath, "I have the possibility of becoming the real Messiah." According to Unification philosophy, that is dependent on the success of Moon and his church in creating a world theocracy.

To do so, the mistakes of the past found in Jesus' failed mission must not be repeated. According to Unification philosophy, Jesus was deserted by most of his followers at the time he needed them most. He did not have the political power to bring about the new age. He stood alone and vulnerable when political enemies confronted him. Because of that, he was crucified. The Perfect Family was never created. Moon, apparently, does not plan to make the same mistakes. Scattered in writings by Moon or attributed to Moon and in speeches and other quoted material are such statements as: "I have a master strategy to win America . . . "; "If we can manipulate seven nations at the least then we can get hold of the whole world . . . "; "We can make senators and congressmen out of our own followers . . . "; " . . . every people, or every organization, that goes against Unification Church will gradually come down, or drastically come down and die . . . " Power. Strategy. Preparedness. Manipulation. Persuasion. Threat. Key words in the foregoing quotations attributed to Moon. To achieve the power to make the strategy work, money is required. A great deal of money. And money is exactly what the Unification Church is now said to have. According to *U.S. News*, May 1982, the value of Unification businesses is estimated at 100 million dollars. It owns prestigious real estate in New York City, New York State and California, two newspapers, and in recent years has been buying into the fishing industry. Moon lives in luxury on a $700,000 estate on the Hudson River in Irvington, New York. His suc-

Followers of Sun Myung Moon, carrying posters and American flags, gathered outside the U.S. district courthouse in New York, while inside Moon pleaded not guilty to the charge of filing false income tax returns.

cessful quest for power is obvious. Somehow during newly elected President Reagan's swearing in, Moon managed to be seated in a section "reserved for guests of the President, the Vice-President and Congress."

Moon has no intention of ignoring the necessity of a strong power-base from which to operate. Jesus might have made the mistake of being vulnerable, but he won't. At least, that is the justification the Unification Church uses when questioned about Moon's real ends. So politically active is Moon and his church that the sincerity of his "religious" purposes is now strongly in question. In *Beloved Son*, Steve Allen quotes a 1978 Sub-Committee Report from the House of Representatives in which Moon is reported to have said, "Separation between religion and politics is what Satan likes most." Moon believes that religion cannot be victorious without politics. Religion and politics must be one. On the other hand, if his critics are correct, religion may merely be a tool to achieve political power.

Gifts of Deceit by Robert Boettcher and Gordon L. Freedman is perhaps the best source for a thoroughly documented, exhaustive study of Moon and the Unification Church. Critical of Moon's use of followers to build an empire, to bring large amounts of money into the United States, and to import Koreans to work for the church as "religious trainees," the book makes clear that there are dangers inherent in the First Amendment and that Moon is using freedom of religion to get around the law. Far more frightening are the alleged connections between Moon and the South Korean government. There are accusations that Moon has been instrumental in promoting the interests of the Korean government here in the United States.

Moon's followers may be as many as three million worldwide. Forty thousand live in the United States. His recruiting techniques have been widely criticized, especially in that the Unification Church often uses "front" organizations to initiate the interest of potential recruits. Further discussion of these methods may be found in Chapter Six, on recruiting.

Moon has not been without problems, and in recent years those problems have increased. He applied for membership in the National Council of Churches but was turned down. And the Unification Church's theological seminary in Barrytown, New York, was denied accreditation as a graduate school of theology.

According to *U.S. News and World Report,* May 31, 1982, a House subcommittee studying Moon's activities has said that in Moon's efforts to gain wealth, the church has "systematically violated tax, immigration, banking, currency and Foreign Agents' Registration Act laws as well as state and local laws governing charity fraud."

Time magazine, October 26, 1981, quoted Mose Durst, president of the U.S. branch of the Unification Church as saying that the government is harassing the church. It is possible that the Unification Church, has, at present, more worries than it originally expected. Recently New York City tax authorities proved that some Unification property in the city should not be exempt from taxation because religion is not the "primary purpose" of the church. Moon and one of his chief aides were indicted in Manhattan for tax evasion and for conspiring to evade federal income taxes and filing false tax returns in 1973, 1974, and 1975. Apparently Moon had deposited approximately $1.6 million in an individual account at the Chase Manhattan Bank and failed to report the $112,000 in interest that was earned. The government maintains that he used this money for personal and business reasons and not for church expenses. Moon was convicted of tax evasion, and that case is now pending before the Supreme Court.

"No problem . . . " said Moon. "The way of public life is that we serve God and we serve humanity." With the record growth of followers, wealth, and power, the Unification Church is perhaps the most powerful cult operating in the United States at this time. If what Unification critics, including a number of vocal ex-Moonies, say is true, the way of public life is not in service of God or humanity, but Sun Myung Moon himself.

CHAPTER FOUR

WHY NOW? THE SIXTIES AND SEVENTIES

Whether we look back with horror on the Peoples Temple mass suicide, or whether we look ahead and consider the startling growth of the Unification Church and Sun Myung Moon's increasing wealth and power, nagging questions about why cults have had such success at this time in America's history beg answers. Why were the sixties and seventies so conducive to the appearance of cults? Will cults continue to grow in the eighties and the nineties? What is it about American society that gives cults such an easy foothold upon the lives of young Americans?

Sigmund Freud, perhaps one of the greatest psychiatrists of all time, once said that "religion is born of the need to make tolerable the helplessness of man." Certainly at no time in history have people felt more helpless than in the twentieth century. One has only to pick up the newspaper or listen to the evening news to hear of constant, frightening problems which have no ready answers.

ALREADY ENOUGH NUCLEAR MISSILES
TO DESTROY EARTH

MORE THIRD WORLD COUNTRIES
DEVELOPING ATOMIC POWER

POLLUTION DESTROYING EARTH
AS WE KNOW IT

INFLATION LEADING TO
GREATEST DEPRESSION EVER

CRIME RATE SPIRALING—
PRISONS BULGING

OIL-RICH COUNTRIES WILL
CONTROL THE WORLD

POLAR ICE CAP MELTING—
NEW ICE AGE IN OFFERING

Whether it is the problems of our cities or the decline of the American farmer, whether it is shortages of food or energy or space, the high cost of housing or government deficits, all news seems to be bad news. It is difficult to consider the staggering problems that face humanity without fearing that the world is on the edge of doom.

In the 1960s, a *Time* magazine cover read "God Is Dead." The implication was not so much that people had stopped believing in God, as that they had stopped believing He would solve our problems. Humanity was alone on earth and whatever happened would happen in spite of or because of humankind's actions. Humanity had given up hope in the power of his spirit to solve problems. Americans were replacing spiritualism with technology.

Technology changed the ways people lived and what they valued. It was not an overnight process, of course, because the Industrial Revolution began in the late eighteenth century. But it was during the mid-twentieth century when Americans started questioning whether our reliance on and pride in the things we could manufacture and buy were really healthy or satisfying. Many began to believe that material things had become so important that a void had been created. That void led to negativism.

The generation of the sixties was more dissatisfied than other generations. It challenged the military and the government over the war in Vietnam. It questioned the value of education. It scoffed at the "work hard, make money" ethics of former generations. It contrasted supposed beliefs in equality with the bigotry and racism it saw. It tested freedom of speech and freedom of assembly with sit-ins, voter registrations in the South, and riots. It created a counterculture, the hippies, to show its disdain for an America it believed was hypocritical, greedy, and self-destructive.

Another factor that encouraged negativism was a growing sense of anonymity, of being faceless and unimportant in a world that could care less about the individual. In work and at home, the individual was losing importance. One's job was no longer a creative act, nor was the product of one's work his own. The assembly line made it impossible for laborers to feel a sense of individual accomplishment. One was just a part of a large machine that pounded out products.

At home, the family institution grew weaker. A majority of mothers worked. Working parents were often required to travel. Time for the family to be together was further lessened by the greater mobility of young people, who, in their cars, spent more and more time away from home. The pressures of modern living, from Little League games to golf tournaments, allowed less time for the family to need the family.

Without that need, the family began to fall apart. In three decades, families headed by a single mother rose from 3.7 million to 7.2 million. Today, one out of every three marriages ends in divorce. One out of every six children growing up spends some time living with only one parent. The instability of broken homes creates identity problems. Close to 50 percent of all American youth will require some psychiatric counseling before maturity, say Stoner and Parke in *All God's Children.* Additionally, three times more people commit suicide now than thirty years ago. In one year, 1974 to 1975, the suicide rate rose 10 percent.

Increased geographic mobility has also added to that growing sense of anonymity by cutting families off from their roots. Less than fifty years ago, most Americans had some sense of geographic origin. Many could pinpoint a family homestead from generations before. Today, sprawling corporations have many plants and subsidiaries, and require employees to constantly transplant themselves to new cities or states. The 1970 census discovered that 20 percent of all American families move each year. For a large part of the population, the consequent loss of friends, of familiar systems, of values and customs, and of continuity in education has made growing up a process done among strangers.

The importance of TV to the individual has increased. Unfortunately, the world the TV portrays is also a lonely, violent place. By the time one reaches eighteen, he or she has witnessed over three thousand acts of violence; has watched a nightly fare of blackmail, fraud, infidelity, rape, and murder; and has passively come to accept atrocity as a part of living. Not only has TV made the seediest aspects of life a reality, it has had other psychologically damaging effects as well. The inability to concentrate, passive involvement, and passive acceptance are three.

Finally, the importance of religion has continued to diminish. Religion in early America was a way of life. The church was the center of activity. Today, for too many Americans, church has become a one-hour Saturday or Sunday obligation.

Cults, on the other hand, inspire with the hollow phrases society has taught individuals to accept. As S. P. Hersh of the National Institute of Mental Health states in "Cults and Youth Today," cults give the convert assurances and absolutes that society does not or cannot give. Cults offer the "one true religion," an absolute for which people yearn in a world in which nothing seems certain. Many promise that one can become a sacred being at a time when one wonders if he or she has any importance at all.

In a society in which the individual no longer believes he is important, cults that profess to value the individual have strong appeal. In a society in which the individual feels helpless, cults claim that each person can help to change the world. If the world seems fraught with insoluble problems, cults offer ready answers. For those who strongly need to believe in a god who has not abandoned them, cults offer a means to relate to God. For those who yearn for stability and a sense of community, the cults claim they have it. It is no wonder that cults have multiplied and flourished in the last two decades. They have gained their strength by playing upon the weaknesses of American society and the needs society today has created in individuals. They offer commitment and service in a world in which there is little opportunity for either. They teach religion and prayer and scriptures to those who often have little real background in their interpretation. They preach against a world they see as evil, materialistic, and greedy. And they offer those who would flee the confusion an escape.

CHAPTER FIVE

WHY YOUNG PEOPLE?

Alone, a college freshman aimlessly wanders the campus. He wonders why he is disappointed, for he worked hard to be accepted. He feels outside the mainstream, caught in the eddies and swirls of a stronger current that seems to be carrying him nowhere. He pauses for a moment on the sidewalk, wishing for the familiar faces of his hometown Main Street. If only they would miraculously replace the anonymous, indifferent glances of the groups that hurry past him. Suddenly he feels a gentle tug at his sleeve, turns, and looks down into the scrubbed, shiny face of a girl with some pamphlets in her hand.

"Hi. My name is Nancy." She smiles. "What's yours?"

A shy girl, invited by two new friends to dinner at their home, snuggles into the corner of a sofa. She is surrounded by several young men and women her age. They seem intrigued by her opinions on society, on education, on just about everything. She feels important and interesting. What delights her most is that what she is saying actually impresses them. She's heady; she's effervescent. "Why haven't I met these people before?" she wonders. "I feel so at home here, like I really belong."

A college senior, nearing graduation, fingers the corporate applications accumulating on his desk. The yellow glow of his desk lamp makes him feel he's an island surrounded by darkness. He's going to be on his own in just one more month. His mother and father expect him to find a good job, especially after so many years of college tuition. He wishes he were just a freshman, but he's not sure why. Beside the empty applications rests the want ads. Circled with spirals and arrows, an hour's doodling, is an advertisement seeking young people to "promote new paths" for the "betterment of mankind."

He runs his finger around the advertisement and then, having made a decision, he pushes the applications aside, grabs the paper, and heads for the pay phone.

During the sixties and seventies, America was ripe for the epidemic growth of cults. Those unhappy with what America had become, those yearning for something worthwhile and satisfying to do with their lives, and those needing something certain and meaningful to hold onto, turned to cults hoping cults had what society lacked. They turned in record numbers, and the cults multiplied.

Although older people did join cults, the great majority were young. Rabbi Maurice Davis, a veteran cult watcher, states that the typical recruit is 18–25, probably upper-middle class, and white. More than likely he or she yearns for "peer approval" and is uncomfortable in a "Permissive society." In some cases, the world seems a bit "too big" for him or she is not sure of herself. Perhaps there is a relationship that just ended or a fear of going off on one's own. In all, Davis says there is a "lot of goodness" and the strong desire "to see a better world in the people cults recruit."

Davis's description makes perfect sense. In the 1960s and 1970s, America came under a lot of criticism from people of all ages. But young Americans were also actively searching for their place in society. While the older generations had found their jobs and started their families, young people were still grappling with questions about who they were and what they wanted to do with their lives. Unfortunately, while America wasn't supplying many answers, the cults were.

It is in adolescence and during the twenties that the individual is most likely to look critically upon his parents, see problems, and decide that his life will be different. One Hare Krishna devotee cited in J. Stillson Judah's *Hare Krishna and the Counterculture* talked about his father:

> His whole thing is devotion to work, just plain work, and he doesn't realize that they're just going to kick him out in another ten years or five years without a care, so it's just misplaced devotion.

Another, describing herself and her family, stated:

> I was miserable . . . I mean, I have a rich family and everything. Everything was there, but it was a miserable situation.

Another, describing his relationship with his father said:

> He wanted me to be an engineer really badly, and I kind of swerved away from that, so he wanted me to be great in the eyes of society. That's the whole thing I'm trying to make him understand isn't the real goal. . . . I told him . . . "We're both suffering, we're both in ignorance, we're both in the material world. We've got to get out. There's no safety here." I said: "You're not really happy here doing what you're doing. You're trying to make me do the same thing." And one time he admitted it. He said: "I know I'm not happy, but you let me be in my unhappiness!"

Maturity requires independence from parents. Yet independence from parents can ony be attained by striking out on one's own. The process of maturing and moving away from the secure environment of childhood, of taking responsibility for oneself, can be lonely or overwhelming. Some young people marry early, finding security in being one of two. Others look for groups to diminish their sense of isolation or distress:

> I was getting crazier and crazier each year and more and more frustrated . . . so what brought me to Krishna Consciousness was complete, overwhelming, undeniable and irrevocable distress.

Across America people read the reports of group marriages, heard of young people leaving their homes and families, opened their doors to find earnest groups soliciting for God, saw flower children wandering the streets and wishing strangers well, were warned of growing drug abuse, and decided that certainly the generation of the sixties was missing something— a sense of responsibility or, in the extreme, any shred of sanity.

Generally, these young people were a part of the hippie movement, long-haired and rootless, distrustful of society and critical of established values and customs. Establishment society regarded them distrustfully, too. The stereotype continued well into the seventies. As far as society was concerned, only those on the boundaries or beyond the ken of the sane and stable joined cults.

Any new movement attracts psychologically unstable people, people whose problems in coping with reality predispose them to joining fringe groups. Certainly, the cults' appeal is strong for these individuals. But by the seventies, America began to realize that the cults were also attracting normal young people in greater and greater numbers. With that realization, Americans also realized that cults, if they were dangerous, were a far more serious threat than formerly imagined.

Young people between the ages of nineteen and twenty-six are particularly vulnerable to cults. They are no longer children and they are not yet fully adults. Their childlike innocence has been discarded, but they have not yet come to grips with adult realities. The values that they accepted from their parents have been cast aside, but new values, based on their own experiences, are still being formed. They are in transition.

Often, in order to fill the void created by the rejection of childhood beliefs and values, young people grab ready-made replacements that are wrong for them. The cult can function as substitute parents. The new convert has left home and believes he or she is living independently. There is no need for questions about what to do; a code of behavior is given everyone by the cult. The new convert can relate to the opposite sex with certainty because the cult determines how everyone must behave. The convert can relax about being successful, achieving in a world of intense competition, because in the cult, people function as part of a group rather than as individuals. Tasks of new cult members are generally unchallenging. They no longer need to agonize over decisions or critically evaluate their thinking. They need only obey. If they doubted their own capabilities, they need only be obedient and they will be accepted, praised, and even loved.

CHAPTER
SIX

RECRUITING
TECHNIQUES

Cults have a ready market in young people, and they capitalize on it. If it is loneliness, the need for approval, or the need for an authority figure to replace parental authority; if it is an overwhelming fear of one's unimportance in the universe, a soured love affair, or any one of hundreds of variations of unfulfilled dreams, cults step in at times when the individual is most vulnerable, to supply answers, fill voids, and offer hope.

One cult boasts it has found Truth. Another claims that perfection is attainable. One guru claims he has made contact with the inner essence of all living things. He tells his followers to seek Truth and they will find it. Those who believe that Truth is something graspable, listen and obey.

Cults recruit in many different ways, but all depend upon and use followers to increase their numbers. An ex-Moon disciple, Christopher Edwards, writes that even before he was a completely convinced convert, he was already spouting Moon philosophy to the newest of recruits and practicing upon them the recruiting methods that had been used upon him. Recruiting is a way of life for most cultists, something done every day, and for some, all day, while they remain in the cult.

In many cults, training for recruiting is as sophisticated and scientific as the sales training programs used by industry. Recruiters do not waste time on bad prospects. They are trained to recognize good prospects for recruitment through certain signs—especially signs of rootlessness, which betray an individual in a state of transition. Backpacks and suitcases, lonely or frightened expressions, the lost look of someone in a new city—all are "green lights" to recruiters. They gather outside counseling centers, registration centers, and bus terminals. On college campuses they focus on college freshmen and seniors. They look for graduates without jobs, or wanderers between jobs. They want vulnerable individuals, people who are looking for something, not those who are happy with what they have or what they are doing.

Get them talking. That's one of the techniques used during initial contact. Listen. Agree with everything. Be helpful. Make the potential recruit think he or she is special. One doesn't have to be young or fearful or uncertain to find such flattery turning one's head. Everyone enjoys feeling important, exciting, or brilliant. It's very difficult to dislike people who come on so positively. It takes a hardened cynic to question the motives of people who seem so genuinely interested in you.

Often recruiters are careful to match potential recruits with members of the opposite sex, introducing a whole new dimension to the appeal of the cult. Many ex-cultists remember sensing that their recruiters might be romantically interested in them. By the time they realized that such was not the case, they were already entrenched in the group. In some cases, as with Children of God, female recruiters are told by their leader, Moses Berg, to be "flirty fish." Making eye and body contact with a potential recruit to arouse him sexually, is an extremely effective selling ploy.

Another useful recruiting technique establishes strong feelings of identifying with the recruit. It is not coincidental that recruiters often have an amazingly similar background to that of the recruit.

Having been asked to dinner by a Unification Church recruiter the first night he was in Berkeley, California, Chris

Edwards noticed how the people in his circle "seemed to hang onto every word," how extremely interested they were in his reasons for being in Berkeley, his studies, and his interests. Eventually he found them probing more, especially in the area of religious background. Later he noticed "a peculiar pattern" developing—whenever he answered their questions, others in the group would point out how much alike his life or feelings were to theirs. "They seemed to be playing upon my identity, deliberately trying to draw me close," Edwards writes. Identifying with the recruit establishes a sense of bond, a closeness that is useful when recruiting.

If the recruit grew up in the Mid-West, had trouble being the oldest child, lost his mother when he was young, or had trouble relating to his father, more than likely one of those assigned to the recruit will also "coincidentally" be from the Midwest, the oldest, and raised by a single parent. The natural human need to share experiences and to be understood makes this technique especially effective.

Some cults are clear about their recruiting purposes from the beginning. Some are not. The Unification Church has communal centers in 120 cities; it recruits on at least 150 college campuses. Recruiting is absolutely necessary to the future of the movement. It is notorious for often deceiving a potential recruit until the recruit is sufficiently ensnared in the movement. Recruiters do not mention Sun Myung Moon's name. They do not refer to the Unification Church. Names such as the Creative Community Project, a front organization for the church, or the Collegiate Association for Research of Principle, or some other lofty academic or scientific, but not religious, name is often used. In this way, potential recruits who might

*A Moon follower, hoping
to attract new recruits,
hands out literature on
a New York City street.*

otherwise be wary of the cult can be lulled into joining a group they would likely have rejected.

Most often, the recruit's initial contact with the cult seems a chance one, a twist of fate. The potential recruit is invited to dinner and a lecture at the home of the recruiter. There the recruits and other guests are showered with attention and made to feel special. They see all the recruiter's friends living in harmony, something directly in contrast to the alienation and loneliness they feel. Usually a short lecture follows dinner, one predictably based upon building a better world. The lecturer is either a member of the household, called "The Family" in the Unification Church, or an honored visitor from out of town. His talk is inspirational and the recruits' idealism and sense of purpose are aroused. The lecture may be followed by group singing and more friendly conversation. Chris Edwards likens the moment to "a Georgia tent revival," "all sweetness and light," yet he enjoyed "the sense of innocence." He came away believing that the cult wanted to "increase human understanding so that all men may live in harmony."

Yearning for understanding themselves, many recruits are easy prey for such platitudes. If they are among "Moonies," they are invited to a weekend workshop. If a recruit is at first not interested or begs to postpone participating in this second step, he can expect friendly phone calls to continue until he either gives in or becomes a waste of time to his recruiter. He may be "honored" by being personally invited by one of the cult's directors. The calls will urge him on with additional invitations to dinner or some other event, all in the name of friendship. But the weekend is the crucial step for the Unification Church.

The weekend consists of activities which critics of cults and ex-cultists claim employ intensive pressure tactics or brainwashing. Some reporters and others interested in the purposes and aims of cults such as the Unification Church have participated in these weekends and have expressed at the end their astonishment at how easily persuaded they were, how close they came to being converted. While these were people who knew exactly what was going to happen, most recruits have no idea what to expect, nor do they know that they have become the subject of tried and proven persuasion techniques. With their new friends, they climb on buses for a weekend retreat that they think will be a lark.

They are asked to join hands to create a better world. And join hands they do. The weekend is nonstop caring and constant activity. Surrounded by recruiters, often even accompanied to the bathroom, potential recruits haven't a moment to themselves. Lectures on God's purpose, on despair, or on the chance for salvation are interspersed with calisthenics, games, singing, and confessional sessions. Through the latter, the cults gain more information about the recruits' guilts, fears, and needs by encouraging them to ask questions and to open up about their feelings. They use this information to further relate to recruits and to sell them on joining.

Although recruits climb on the bus together, they never talk alone again. The Unification Church takes no chances that a cynical visitor might divert others who are moving along nicely toward conversion. In his book, *Crazy for God,* Chris Edwards remembers how one boy who arrived with him was gone the next day. When he asked his whereabouts, Edward's guide said he had been asked to leave. Apparently he was too "negative."

Some, the smarter ones, recognize what's behind this weekend. Although it is still unlikely that Moon's name is mentioned, they pick up clues. Others do not and actually come home from the weekend still unaware of the religious nature of the group they are now very likely to join.

Near the end of the weekend, recruits are urged to sign up for the week-long workshop. It is a hard sell. After such intensive persuasion, few are capable of refusing. They feel an obligation to their new friends. They think that the group is something special. They feel wanted, even needed. All weekend, they have listened to how evil and corrupt the world is. They do not want to deny themselves the chance to make it better.

The techniques the Unification Church uses follow what

some psychologists consider a classic pattern of antagonism, apathy, and acceptance, according to Joel MacCollam in *Carnival of Souls*. The recruits may come to the week-long session still in control of their own destiny, antagonistic to giving themselves to a cause, and skeptical of platitudes about making a better world. Edward's first impression of the Moonies he met was that despite obvious friendliness, their "smiling faces" troubled him. Especially their eyes, which he described as "glassy, like two eggs sunny-side up . . ." He recognized a hollowness in the lectures he attended, perceiving that the lecturer "did not understand a good deal of what he had said." When asked a question, the lecturer would "respond by mouthing slogans from his talk."

Chris Edwards recognized the nature of the recruitment process. He knew the recruiters were "professional proselytizers" even if he wasn't sure what their goals truly were. Yet he had no idea "what the end result might be".

The end result for Edwards was seven months in the Unification Church. Had he not been kidnapped by his father and deprogrammed by Ted Patrick, perhaps the most famous anticult activist in the United States, he might still be there.

If Edwards began as a skeptic, how did the Unification Church manage to turn him into a convinced convert? Anyone who has ever been exposed to endless people and activity can remember the resultant fatigue of both mind and senses. Humans need time to themselves to organize their thoughts and to relax. Even the time to remain calm and unmoved is invaluable in regaining a sense of oneself as an individual.

Those moments are nonexistent during the intensive recruiting programs used by many cults. Often, time to go to the bathroom, to eat, and to sleep are put off or severely curtailed. Some who have been on Unification retreats charged that the diet, high in carbohydrates, is purposefully planned to induce elated feelings, "sugar highs," at essential moments and fatigue and apathy, "sugar lows," at other crucial times. In the apathetic state, recruits become increasingly vulnerable to pressure. It is almost as if they will accept anything for relief. And accept they do. In record numbers each year.

Geographically removed from the distractions of the real world and the reality of obligations and friends, from the clues of familiar faces and surroundings that keep humans in touch with reality, the strange new world of the cult grows more believable and the old world more alien. An extreme of this phenomenon are victims of kidnapping who eventually identify with their captors. Patty Hearst's saga with the Symbionese Liberation Army is one example. Photographed in a bank holdup in which she helped her captors commit their crime, Patty Hearst had become a willing member of the very group that had abducted and tortured her.

Alienation from the real world is also induced by the preaching of most cults. They see the world as evil. Salvation can only occur by following the cult, perhaps even severing all ties with friends and family.

These beliefs contribute to a growing estrangement from the evil influence of the recruit's former life. When Edwards felt an urge to get away for a while, his request was denied. He was told he was "ripe for Satan's attacks . . . Satan will actually get into your mind and possess you." Should he want to take a train, "Satan will derail the train. He's out to get you for sure."

The new convert, physically, emotionally, socially, and intellectually, relinquishes old ties by being cut off from the very anchors of his old life. He is cast adrift and caught in a new current—life in the cult. As with Christopher Edwards, each new recruit believes he is making a conscious decision. Few have any idea what that decision will mean to their futures.

CHAPTER SEVEN

MIND CONTROL

After his first few days with the Unification Church, Chris Edwards was shocked when he looked in the mirror. He didn't look like the same person. He noticed his eyes "were wide as a child's." Although frightened, he began thinking that this "glassy stare" was "God's way of setting people apart, distinguishing His chosen people." In *Hostage to Heaven,* Betty Underwood, the mother of another "Moonie," noticed a change in her daughter's voice. It had a flatness, a droning quality which frightened her. Other parents and friends of cult recruits are astounded by dramatic changes in the recruit's personality. They notice an inability to think clearly or to concentrate. It's as if the mind and soul have left the body and another being has replaced them.

So dramatic are the changes that many fear something dreadfully wrong is being done within the cults. Others scoff, insisting that the reason for these changes is conversion—a phenomenon very much a part of all religions. Conversion, they claim, is a change in character in which one turns away from one's former, "evil" life to a righteous one. One might convert, then, to Catholicism or Judaism, adopting the beliefs and practices of the new religion and casting aside the beliefs and practices of one's old life. When that happens, the convert may appear to be a different person to those who knew him or her before. And because the new convert is most comfortable and feels most accepted among others who believe as he or she does, family and friends may be avoided or even rejected.

Religious conversion is but one of the theories that can be used to explain the effect cults are having upon recruits. No one is absolutely sure as to what is happening, but a growing number of people, among them many psychiatrists, psychologists, parents, and clergy—believe that cultists are being manipulated through "brainwashing," or "mind control."

Mind control is something abhorrent to most Americans. Americans value independence and individuality. They do not like to think that the individual can be made a puppet without his or her consent. They do not like to think that free will can be taken away or that an individual would willingly give it away. And yet events in the 1950s proved otherwise.

When the Korean War ended and American prisoners of war were released, Americans were shocked to find that these prisoners had not even attempted to escape from their captors. Equally shocking was that they came home with a violent hatred of America and its values. They voiced their hatred in the same phrases and terms used in Communist propaganda. Worst of all, many had no desire to return to their families. When psychiatrists and psychologists were called in to help these POWs readjust to American society, they became more and more certain that the Chinese had used pressure techniques to break down or bury their prisoners' former personalities.

These techniques were characterized by several things. Prisoners were subjected to violence or the threat of violence. Torture, or the threat of it, created constant stress. That stress was heightened by isolation. Not only were the prisoners isolated from old friends and values, they were frequently moved from one place to another, prohibiting the development of new friendships and making readjustment to unfamiliar surroundings a constant necessity. They were given little sleep and a poor diet. All contributed to a kind of disorientation, an uncertainty and instability. This undermined their capacity to resist, to hold onto memories of who they were, what they were, and what they believed.

Having created instability, their captors then monopolized their attention, giving them little or no time to think and scheduling so many activities that they became further exhausted. They ridiculed their captives' beliefs and made them guilty about once having them. At the same time, they pressured prisoners to believe their Communist ideology. In essence, they divided prisoners against themselves, and the POWs, with little stamina to resist, began to believe in their captors and hate America. Once they did, they received seemingly sincere affection, emotional support, and approval. Soon the POWs *wanted* to belong to the very group that had been the enemy.

According to Stoner and Parke, Wes Davis, an instructor at the LESS Anti-Terrorist Academy in Springfield, Illinois, maintains that brainwashing is rare in the West. It requires physical abuse and potential death. Brainwashing is traumatic and severe. Without these elements, it cannot be accomplished. Certainly, there is a wide difference between men captured by the enemy, men who are belligerent and prepared to resist, and those young Americans who join cults. Yet those who voluntarily visit a cult are obviously looking for something they think the cult might offer. Perhaps cults have no need to use physical force or violence with their recruits. Recruits, by their very nature, have already expressed a strong willingness to be convinced, something POWs did not.

Physical violence, then, may only be necessary in the brainwashing process if the subject is hostile. If he is not, if he is already inclined to believe, violence may be unnecessary. Group pressure, combined with the individual's need to conform, is perhaps as serviceable as violence for "convincing" the recruit to stay. One young man, cited in *All God's Children,* remembers his morning with the Unification Church. Having been awakened at 5:30 by a guitarist singing "You Are My Sunshine," he recalls how everybody went along with it. At first he thought they were crazy, but then he began singing too, doing what they were doing. "Either they weren't crazy, or I was. So I decided that they were okay." He began acting like a Moonie, regardless of his skepticism.

Chris Edwards, in *Crazy for God,* remembers how skeptical he was at the first of the lectures to which all recruits are subjected. The speaker maintained that people are so "arrogant" that they fail to recognize Truth; they lack the humility to listen. Yet Edwards' desire to be a part of a "communal framework" made him want to believe. "The desire to belong and work for something 'worthy' eliminates the need to break down resistance. Resistance does not exist."

In addition to the recruit's acknowledged desire to find something, some purpose, some goal for which to work, cults also use intense emotional pressure quite the opposite of violence. They create what is called a "contact high," a phenomenon that occurs frequently in all our lives. It comes from being in contact with people who are joyous and loving. It alters the mood almost by "rubbing off" on others nearby. Cults carefully create a sense of being "high" throughout the recruitment process. They shower recruits with attention and approval. In the Unification Church, it is called "love bombing." The implication is that one can be conquered through love. In many cases, that is exactly what happens. The "high" may also be enhanced by the attention of someone of the opposite sex who seems genuinely to be interested in the recruit. Compounded by less sleep and the "sugar high" diet mentioned in Chapter Three, this phenomenon can create an intense emotional situation that is highly persuasive.

In the early sixties, Robert J. Lifton, one of the experts called in to help POWs adjust after the Korean War, published *Thought Reform and the Psychology of Totalism.* In it, he explained the conditions of "coercive persuasion" or "brainwashing." He called the first condition "milieu control." Put simply, those who wish to persuade surround the recruit with only those people and things that are helpful in the persuasion process. The cult recruit is cut off from the outside world. Newspapers and television are often forbidden. Only people who believe as the cult believes communicate with the recruit.

The second state, "mystical manipulation," inspires with idealism. Cults are working to save the world or to bring inner peace or pursuing some other lofty goal. It is the individual's responsibility to seek these goals. He or she has a chance to be among the Chosen. Lifton's third condition, "the need for purity," develops the idea that to work for a better world, one must face his or her own guilt for having been part of it. The person feels shame for the things he or she has done within that impure world. This creates the need for confession, which is the fourth condition. Recruits tell their innermost secrets and share with the "brainwasher" their fears and anxieties. Barbara Underwood wrote in her journal at about this time:

> My standards for my life have been such narrow ones when I compare them to perfection. And all this time God loved me even while I refused the leap of faith that creates our relationship. . .

Chris Edwards remembers being asked to participate in the writing of a song or skit for presentation to the audience at his weekend encounter. The purpose was to explain the loneliness of his life before meeting the family. Others were asked to do the same thing and Edwards noticed how they "seemed reluctant to express . . . [things they] . . . may not have even believed."

When the recruit reaches this stage, he has been prepared for what will follow. It is what Lifton calls "the aura of sacred science." The "brainwasher" is teaching Truth. It is sacred and beyond questioning. Cults constantly use this technique. Recruits are told that skepticism only shows how little they know. They must accept the word of others. Only in this way can they possibly ever achieve their goal. The "science" is presented in such a way that old words take on new meanings, and that jargon further confuses recruits. They struggle with meanings that others understand easily. Even old songs often have new words which they try quickly to learn so that they can please everyone by singing them robustly. Finally, they learn that the philosophy, the cult doctrine, takes precedence over everything they have learned in life. It is a new world, a new reality, in which they will function. In what Lifton calls "the dispensing of existence," recruits also learn that they are now among those who will be saved. All others are doomed. This completes the alienation from the outside world.

Jim Jones used six generally accepted brainwashing techniques. He isolated his followers in his Guyana camp, set up rigid schedules to which followers had to be totally obedient, and set up daily "study" groups to drill followers in his philosophy. Those who resisted could expect torture, and those who abided by his word were rewarded with freedom and group approval. He also held interrogation sessions in which members who might have been critical confessed. He led his followers to a "promised land" and made them believe that the world was out to destroy them. The world was evil; they were good. They were the Chosen.

Although those who come to the cults are already predisposed to joining, few willingly sacrifice their freedom knowing exactly why they are making that choice and what the final consequences will be. Often the recruit is blind to the goal the cult has for him or her. Consent is obtained in stages, each stage revealing just a little more of what is in store when the "conversion" is complete. Richard Delgado, a faculty member at the University of Washington, whose article, "Limits to Proselytizing," appeared in *Society* magazine, uses a telling analogy to illustrate the techniques many cults employ. A surgeon requests permission to examine a sore on a patient's leg. Then, seeing that it is slightly infected, he asks for permission to apply an antiseptic. Looking more closely, he asks if he may anesthetize the infected area and receives further consent. Discovering cancerous tissue and wishing to get at it immediately, he asks permission to remove the growth. Although the patient is fearful, she too wants it removed and consents. Before she is finished, the patient has lost her leg.

This is, of course, an absurd situation. The point is that the patient did not hesitate to call her doctor about an innocuous sore, but she most certainly would have hesitated had she known her leg would be amputated, even if that did save her life. Decisions based on the final outcome were made in stages, not with full knowledge of the end result.

The same is true for many of those who join cults. Ex-Moonies such as Chris Edwards emphasize that in the beginning, they had no idea that the appealing group recruiting them was even religious, let alone connected with the Unification Church. Ex-members of Children of God have stated they did not know its sexual practices. The problem is one of consent. It is one thing to consent to having one's leg examined and quite another to having it removed. It is one thing to consent to work for world peace and quite another to consent to rejecting parents, friends, worldly goods, and individual freedom. One ex-cultist cited in *All God's Children,* remembered how she had gasped when she learned her group was part of the Unification Church. She couldn't believe that she was a Moonie. Yet, by that time she was "so charged up about saving the world that [she doubts she] would have left on her own."

The change that occurs in the recruit is also gradual. Stoner and Parke in *All God's Children* note that often the recruit starts behaving long before he actually begins believing. Such was certainly the case with Chris Edwards.

Mind control can take many forms. "Brainwashing" in its purest form is the most extreme. But manipulation of individuals can be achieved using a patchwork of several effective persuasive techniques. One is hypnotism. One expert, psychologist James McConnel, claims he can alter anyone's behavior from what it would be to what someone else might want it to be. Frederick Marcuse in a book called *Hypnotism: Fact and Fiction* cites a scientifically controlled experiment in which a strong-willed, articulate, aggressive, confirmed atheist was hypnotically induced into a religious state. It took only three sessions before the experiment had to be stopped—the man was attending church and communicating his new beliefs in God to others.

Joel MacCollam in *Carnival of Souls* calls it "nonholy" conversion in which the change is created not by spiritual experiences but by trained, strong leaders employing a battery of effective ploys. In *Snapping: America's Epidemic of Sudden*

Personality Change, authors Conway and Siegelman see that radical change occuring at what they call a "snapping point," which occurs after the individual has been subjected to intensive pressure, dominating personalities, and emotional frenzy. Whatever the theory, however, whether it is the Korean "brainwashing" that Lifton describes, or hypnotism, or "non-holy conversion," or "snapping," individuality can obviously be undermined by those who are cunning and skillful. The individual can be placed at the mercy of those in control.

That he willingly submits to the process makes the chances of being victimized all the more certain. Chris Edwards describes cult life as "a one-way passage through a dark and seemingly endless tunnel." He notes that in his seven months with the Unification Church, he saw only one member outspokenly spurn Unification beliefs, and leave on his own. A few others ran away or were taken home because "cult life made them too physically or emotionally ill to continue." The rest of those who left were deprogrammed.

There is no question that the mind control techniques detailed in this chapter exist and are extremely effective. Although all cults experience a high turnover, a fact that many cults use to undermine the mind control charges levelled against them, too many ex-cultists have attested to their use for these charges not to have some validity. The public should not ignore the strong possibility that some cults may be doing something very dangerous. Stoner and Parke note that often those who are removed from the cult demonstrate an "inability to function in society without the group's help." Decision making becomes an impossibility. They cited one girl who spent two hours in a store merely trying to choose a few pairs of socks. She just could not make up her mind. John G. Clark, Jr., M.D., Assistant Clinical Professor of Psychiatry at Harvard Medical School, when speaking to the Vermont State Legislature in August, 1976, told of his experiences with long-term cult members. He compared their state to that of an untreated schizophrenic whose illness becomes "acculturated and permanent." Dr. Clark believes "this new style of thinking may become irreversible."

CHAPTER EIGHT

CULT LIFE

Most of the cults cited in this book are communal—that is, followers live together either in urban houses or on farms or ranches. Living with other cultists eliminates many problems. Cults stand a far better chance of keeping followers if they make the cult a way of life. The stronger the bonds between members and the more the follower relies on the cult for his or her social, emotional, and intellectual needs, the more alienated from the outside world he or she feels. The outside world can distract members from their new goals and undermine the influence the cult has worked so diligently to have upon them. The outside world, then, becomes an "enemy" from which cults carefully "protect" the recruit. Jim Jones told Al and Jeannie Mills, two of his early followers: "It's time for you to cut your family ties. This church is your family now. Blood ties are dangerous because they prevent people from being totally dedicated to the cause."

Jones wasn't the first leader to demand such sacrifice. Commitment to a movement and its leader can be endangered by family obligations if the family has not adopted the same beliefs. To be complete, commitment requires all the recruit's thinking and energy. For the cultist, the pursuit of the ideal, the goal of world peace, the unification of religions, the saving of souls from damnation, or following the disciplined paths to Truth requires time and extraordinary energy. The recruit feels responsible and is encouraged so that he or she does not falter in strength of convictions or willingness to sacrifice all. Recruits are also encouraged to be role models for those yet to be converted, those yet to be "chosen," and those yet to be saved. To accomplish this, cults often encourage the severing of all ties, even those with the family.

The break with the family is frequently so complete that most of the well-known cults have been accused by critics of intentionally attempting to break down the family, humankind's strongest and most durable institution. In some cases, the accusations are true. Moses Berg asked:

> Is breaking up families anything new with God? God is in the business of breaking up families—little private families! If you have not forsaken your husband and wife for the Lord at some time or other, you have not forsaken all!

Berg's extremes voice something implicit in many cults' concept of the worldly family. In many cases, cults maintain it is precisely that life of the family which has left the recruit uncertain or unhappy. Yet Berg's stand on families is as absolute and inflexible as much of his theology. Berg said:

> Parents are [the] rotten, decadent, decrepit, hypocritical, self-righteous, inflexible, affluent, self-satisfied, proud, stubborn, disobedient, blind, blood-thirsty, Godless, dead, selfish, churchy, older generation.

It is, of course, the family that stands the greatest chance of recovering one entangled in a cult. By convincing a convert to reject his or her family, the cult accomplishes several things: first, it undermines its strongest enemy; second, it creates an emotional void that was once filled by the family. The new recruit's yearning for a sense of belonging, of being loved, and of being part of something are increased. Then the cult can fill that void. "We are your family. We are your parents," is the essential message of the Unification Church, the Love Israel family, and others. It was also Jim Jones's.

Those left behind, the family and old friends, are usually confused or even angry when the new convert calls or writes to tell them he or she will not be coming home. Many parents immediately try to find their son or daughter and, if they can, try to convince him or her to come home. They look suspiciously upon their offspring's new friends, and are often enraged when they hear that these people have become a new "family." Such reactions, natural as they may be, tend to widen the gulf between the devotees and their former world.

By turning to the cult and thus increasing the cult's power over their lives, recruits face an existence very different from their old lives. While most came from middle-class backgrounds, they will live a life of poverty. While most grew up in a free environment, they will soon obediently follow the whims of their individual masters. While most were encouraged to be individuals, they will now reject "selfish" desires for the goals of the group. While most questioned life as they saw it, they will now learn that questioning is "negative" and that blind acceptance is the only way to achieve happiness.

Their devotion to their masters, whether it is the Maharaj Ji or Sun Myung Moon, must be complete. It is a devotion that allows no skepticism. It is an emotional, social, and intellectual dependence. Stoner and Parke in *All God's Children* watched members of an ashram they had previously visited, an ashram that seemed quite wholesome and sane, sob hysterically when the Marahaj Ji visited. As Maharaj Ji has said: "You cannot battle the mind. It is too complex, too sophisticated. You'll lose. To beat the mind you must ignore it."

Ignore they do. *All God's Children* cites a "supposedly prominent writer for Krishna" who dutifully and complacently explained to the authors "Do you know that if cow slaughter ended, the bad weather in Chicago would change and the temperature rise at least 10 degrees?" No wholesome flicker of skepticism crossed her face as she related this incredible "fact." Krishnas, of course are vegetarians. Eating meat is sinful. But she was perfectly willing to let a dietary taboo explain the weather of a city because her swami had told her so.

The more devoted and unquestioning the convert, the better. Several ex-cultists have noticed that among cult members a kind of competition to be the most blindly obedient develops. Christopher Edwards describes a scene in which family members joined in prayer by touching their faces to the carpet. Their voices grew louder and louder until Edwards "realized that each heavenly child was repeating his personal prayer for others to hear." It was, he says, an "uncanny competition . . . [in which each tried] . . . to outdo the other in righteousness, volume, and emotional force."

For their acceptance cultists gain love and praise. They are criticized severely, and are considered "negative," if they have questions. Dedicating oneself absolutely, putting aside thoughts of oneself and one's selfish desires, and erasing from one's memory concepts one previously held will result in God's love and help, Edwards was told.

Devoting himself to God meant that for awhile, Edwards helped to "process" new recruits and then to work on the Unification Church's Mobile Fund Raising Team. Although most members maintain that their fund raising is done primarily to support their operations and that the public has widely exaggerated the millions they supposedly accrue, fund raising is the most important priority of many cults. It is a major part of each devotee's life, requiring sacrifice, hard work, determination and perseverance. Cults make it the best way for a devotee to prove himself sincere and worthy, and the best way to gain praise and status from other cult members.

In the Unification Church, those who are assigned to fund raising teams do intensive work for several weeks, traveling from city to city on buses or in vans. Often these young people go for days without showers, sleeping in their vehicles and eating short order fast foods as a steady diet. One cultist cited in *All God's Children* stated that he lived with six others in an unheated van while soliciting with the Mobile Fund Raising Team. Together they spent a mere $130.00 a week on necessities, yet they raised $7,000.00 per week for the cult. Christopher Edwards' group amassed a similar amount which the bus driver quickly deposited at local banks. *Hostage to Heaven,* written by ex-cultist Barbara Underwood and her mother, Betty, notes that in a nine-month period in 1976, her six member Mobile Fund Team made $450,000 selling roses. Additionally, the Underwoods note testimony in 1977 from one ex-cultist that five million dollars was collected nationwide in a one-month period. The Unification Church has mustered probably the most successful army of fund raising workers, but the Children of God and Hare Krishna have also found similar fund-raising efforts successful. Apparently, money must only be the "root of all evil" when it is in the wrong hands, or cults would not spend so much time extracting it from the public and putting it in their own hands.

Unfortunately, fund raising by its very nature tends to further support the cult's view of the world as greedy, uncaring, or evil. Many communities have tried to make it difficult for cults to solicit, requiring permits and throwing fundraisers in jail for the night if they do not have one. Door-to-door fund raisers quickly learn that canvassing for donations results in all manner of rebuffs, from slammed doors to angry outbursts. Female fund raisers, encouraged to face every challenge, have found themselves in embarrassing if not dangerous circumstances in bars and on street corners. Those who daily face such treatment grow even more certain that the outside world is the devil's workshop.

Cults have been accused of placing too much emphasis on making money and of immoral, if not illegal, fund raising techniques. Jim Jones believed that in order for the church to support its members and its operations, deceit was necessary. Not only did he mislead through faith healing, he also illegally manipulated the government's welfare system through foster care and nursing home fraud and the illegal garnering of older members' social security checks. Those who raise funds for many cults learn to use whatever method is most successful, regardless of whether it is honest or not. Often solicitors lie about the organization for which they are fund raising, evading questions and implying connections with traditionally accepted religions and social organizations. Perhaps the funds are for "the new Bible school" upstate. Perhaps they are for some "foundation." Whatever the supposed purpose, many cultists play upon the charity and good nature of an unsuspecting public for their own ends.

The very deceits that, in Jones's eyes, made the world evil are allowable if used for good. That same philosophy has been adopted by other cults. In *Crazy for God*, Chris Edwards writes of how he once questioned Keith, another fund raiser, about telling people that they were donating money for needy children. The reply was that it was Heavenly Deception, "not Satan's deception . . ." As he saw it, it was "turning Satan against himself."

Loyalty to leader and to cause are top priorities. Devotion means placing long-range goals, good goals according to the cult, before honesty or sincerity. Joel MacCollam in *Carnival of Souls* cites one testimony:

> I was told to lie to those people we were trying to enlist or those from whom we tried to raise funds. I was told that I shouldn't ever say that we were with our group or connected with (our leader). Any possible means for getting money or people was justified on the grounds that the whole world outside was evil and satanic.

In *Beloved Son*, Steve Allen writes that certain Children of God devotees clearly stated in a national telecast that "they had a right to lie, cheat, steal and even murder, so long as it was for the good of the cause."

Instances in which well-meaning individuals have allowed what they thought lofty ends to justify immoral means are common in history. Hitler, for instance, convinced the German people that his end was a healthy Germany. That millions of Jews and others were murdered to achieve this end is perhaps the blackest of all stains upon the record of humankind. Such justifications are self-corrupting. Jones began with fraud and misrepresentation and essentially ended a murderer.

Synanon members attempted the murder of a lawyer who won a judgment against them. Believing in "anything for the cause," leaders and followers don't know where to stop. Chris Edwards recalled that while being deprogrammed by Ted Patrick, Patrick suggested that he would kill his own parents if Moon requested it. At first Edwards could only turn away, but when Patrick pressed him, he finally murmured, "I'd do anything for Heavenly Father." It may be a gradual process, but eventually believing "ends justify means" results in total amorality.

If a recruit is not fund raising, which for many cultists requires nearly seventy percent of their time, he or she may be completing other assigned tasks. Recruiting is almost as important as raising money, for obvious reasons. The Unification Church, for instance, has an extremely high turnover rate. Nearly one-third of all recruits leave each year. Recognizing a crucial need not only to replace lost workers, but also to increase their numbers, "Moonies" have set up approximately 120 centers across the United States for recruiting purposes.

Other responsibilities vary. One can grow within the organization, receiving something akin to corporate promotions. If leadership is an obvious talent, leadership roles may be assigned. Others are assigned jobs employing their talents if those talents are useful to the organization. Still others are responsible for the menial tasks that must be done to maintain the household, the ranch, or the estate. Synanon assigned the lowliest tasks to the drug users it recruited. Middle-class recruits who had no drug problem were used if their talents matched needs. An architect, for instance, might be in charge of designing a new building. Jones used many of his followers to aid political candidates. Moon, having bought into the fishing industry by setting up centers in Massachusetts, Alabama, Virginia, and California, employs many followers. It is no wonder that cult business ventures turn remarkable profits.

Almost all the cults mentioned so far require members to donate their worldly goods to the cause, and most cultists have no independent income. Those who work outside the cult send a hefty portion of their wages to cult headquarters. Krishnas, for instance, are expected to donate a minimum of 50 percent of their wages. Others, depending on the cult for food and lodging, cannot help but eventually lose sight of who is helping whom. Instead of the pride that comes from aiding a cause, the worker instead loses much of his or her sense of individual purpose, independence, and self-worth. Most cultists believe that they depend on the cult rather than, more precisely, the cult on them. So complete is that dependence that some cultists are not even allowed to touch money. One dissatisfied cultist cited by Stoner and Parke in *All God's Children* wanted to call home but couldn't. She didn't have a dime for the pay phone.

In some cults, medical attention is nonexistent. Illness in many cult philosophies is merely a symptom of a lack of true belief or spiritual purity. In *Crazy for God*, Chris Edwards tells of one woman who showed him a sore on her leg that was covered by black scabs. She claimed it was a way of paying for her sins. Then she told him that another boy, Julian, who was suffering from an extreme case of poison oak, had prayed to "accept responsibility" for Edwards's sins. "You haven't been a good little boy . . . " she said.

Sometimes poor diet creates severe medical problems, as in the case of one fund-raiser, a member of one of Moon's Mobile Fund Raising Teams. Stoner and Parke note that he had to be hospitalized for malnutrition. The Fund Raising Team's diets are among the worst. Others are merely different, vegetarian or highly spiced, as in the cases of Hare Krishna and the Divine Light Mission. The nutritional quality of the cultists' diets varies from cult to cult and even from center to center.

Certain cult rituals may also jeopardize health. The Love Israel Family, which claims Steve Allen's son as one of its members, received tremendous notoriety when two of its members died from sniffing toluene, an industrial solvent, during a "rite of breathing." Additionally, their belief in not touching a dead body for at least three days in case life might be restored created problems with the county coroner's office at the time of the two deaths. Stoner and Parke cited another

Love Israel's practices witnessed by a former member. A circle of devotees held hands while one in the circle held a piece of metal to an electrical outlet. Successively, members left the circle, each time increasing the voltage running through the remaining held hands. The established record of the least number who could remain was two.

Society has long recognized the need for stable family units to prevent chaos and insure its own existence. So has religion. But this is not always true in cult philosophy or practice. Not only do many reject former family ties, but they also do not revere marriage within the cult. In the Love Israel family, previously married couples are encouraged to divorce if one partner's devotion wanes. Paul Erdman, leader of the family, "bonds" two people in marriage as he sees fit. He may also "unbond" should he choose. Marriages in the Love Israel family were originally duly authorized and carried out by the clergy. That is no longer the case, and many marriages have never been registered legally. Scientologists do their own marrying. So does Synanon. Neither are Children of God marriages always registered and some of their "betrothal" practices came under the scrutiny of the attorney general of New York. Apparently one ritual involved the marriage of people who were not aware until that moment that they were to be married. Having joined one couple, Berg asked the guests if anyone else wanted to be married. Several men called out whatever woman's name they pleased. The women had no choice.

The Unification Church considers marriage holy and serious. Several requirements must be met first, including having followed Moon for several years. The goal of Unification marriages is the production of "perfect, sinless children," attainable only if Moon chooses the couples and gives them his marital blessing. His marriage ceremonies are famous. One was held at Madison Square Garden in New York City. Over two thousand couples were married. In that Moon's ultimate goal is a world theocracy, he is careful to blend races and nationalities. Critics, however, question his motives. More than one-half of all Unification marriages unite foreign nationals with U.S. citizens. Many believe that his actual purpose may be to

The Reverend Sun Myung Moon performed a mass wedding for 2,200 couples in Madison Square Garden. His wife is on the left.

obtain for foreigners permanent residence in the United States without dealing with U.S. immigration laws or quotas.

The Krishna marriage, according to Stanley Bernstein, who studied the cult for a doctoral dissertation, is one of the most difficult to maintain. Krishna philosophy sees women as a "drag" on their men, a threat to their attainment of spiritual purity. Women are dealt with strictly—in certain instances— even beaten—should problems arise. Krishnas believe that each time a male engages in sex, he damages brain cells and wastes the energy he needs to attain his goal. Intimate relations are a "duty" to create children. Often married couples live in separate dormitories, staying together only at times when conception is possible. Partners may be sent to different parts of the country for long periods of time, further lessening opportunities for close ties. Krishna philosophy discourages mere sexual gratification; premarital or extramarital relations are strictly taboo.

Krishna marriages are arranged. They have two purposes—to raise Krishna children and to encourage partners to help each other develop Krishna Consciousness. Although divorce is not recognized, male ministers may take the Order of Sannyasa which requires that they separate from their wives. The wives are not allowed to remarry but remain within the protection of the cult.

Cults differ in their stances on chastity. "Moonies" revere chastity. Premarital sex is absolutely forbidden. Even thinking lustful thoughts is a sign of Satan's influence. *Crazy for God* notes that "Moonies" are careful to keep their eyes off others' bodies. Every so often, if a "lusty glimmer" occurs during eye contact, it is followed "by great feelings of guilt, relieved only by hours of tearful carpet-pounding in the prayer room." The other extreme is, of course, the Children of God. As discussed in previous chapters, sex is used as a form of recruitment tool. Sexual gratification involves no sin.

The role of women in cults is generally demeaning. Krishna women must be humble and submissive. As one female Krishna devotee told J. Stillson Judah:

> Well, spiritually we have an equal position. . . .
> We're subordinate now in Kali Yoga, but it doesn't
> mean we're inferior necessarily. Actually we are . . . I
> can see that women tend to flip out a lot more than
> men. They are more emotional. . . . On the whole we
> are less intelligent, our attention is not so good. . . .
> So we take our orders from the men and it's nice . . .
> you don't have to make the decisions; it's really pleas-
> ant. . . .

The woman's appraisal of her role in the cult seems confused.
On the one hand, she wants to say she is equal. On the other,
she accepts the fact that women are not allowed decision-making positions within the cult because they are inferior.

While in Krishna, women are a kind of necessary evil for
the creation of Krishna children, in the Unification Church
women are "the shameful descendants of wicked Eve." Often
their inferior position is emphasized by being the last to be
received by visiting dignitaries. In many cults, women are
assigned the servile work—cooking or cleaning. Their work
does nothing to build the self-confidence and self-esteem that
come with responsibility. In other cults, women have been
used for their leader's sexual purposes. Many women and
young girls who were members of Jones's Peoples Temple
were forced to have sexual relations with him. According to
Kenneth Wooden in *Children of Jonestown* Jones bragged that
"he was the only one who could really satisfy man or woman."
When his wife threatened to leave him after discovering his
infidelities, he claimed that they were for "religious reasons"
but that it "disgusted him." He also made it clear that he
would kill their four children if she dared to go. She made a
public statement:

> I knew I didn't want to lose Jim, so I agreed that I
> would share him with people who needed to relate to
> the Cause on a more personal level. This has been a
> very difficult thing for me to live with. . . . Howev-

er, tonight, as I heard him pour out his heart to you, explaining the suffering he goes through when he has to use his body to serve the Cause, I realized that I have been very selfish.

Sarah Berg, of the Children of God, testified that she was forced to mate with Berg's son and later to marry him. After she had his son's child, the older Berg took an interest in her which she rebuffed. Although pregnant at the time, she was beaten.

Although daily life in cults varies widely, certain characteristics are common to all of them. All attempt to create harmony among members, an awesome task. Personalities naturally clash, with tension the byproduct. Cults try to lessen tension through group sessions, by emphasizing the need for selflessness, and by constantly reminding followers of their end goal, whether it is world theocracy or the attainment of Truth. Many have developed group rituals; others call members together for singing, for chanting, or for dancing. Most have regular daily lectures that reemphasize the importance of practicing as well as believing one's religion. And because most cults have developed clearly defined rules of behavior, many tension-creating situations are avoided.

Cults do not let their members become bored. Most cultists have little time to think with fund raising, "witnessing," working, or attending prayer/lecture sessions eighteen hours a day. Solitary thinking, the kind in which an individual weighs and evaluates what he or she has been doing and learning, is not often encouraged. Movies, television, even books that promote what cults consider "negative" thinking are shunned. Critical thinking can undermine a recruit's progress toward total obedience. Chris Edwards noted a kind of sloganism in the Unification Church. "No more concepts," "You think too much," "Your mind is fallen," and other phrases were repeated until they involuntarily became his thoughts.

Their group life is largely supportive. The cult is careful to make the individual feel needed and worthy. Everyone is loved. Some may eventually wonder how love given so freely and equally can possibly make them special. Some may question the futility of trying to change the world by singing or selling flowers or begging money door to door. Practicing a religion that requires rejection of one's former life and complete commitment does, for some, become tiring or humdrum. Some become disenchanted with the sincerity of their leader and look elsewhere for fulfillment. If certain testimonies given by angry ex-cultists are true, perhaps the sudden realization that one is being used for the leader's monetary or power quests leads to rejection of the cult. Whatever the reasons, a high turnover of cult members is well documented.

Those who remain, and many do, grow more distant from the world they once knew. They are isolated in their dormitories and their communes. They contact the outside world only to get something from it—money or recruits. In many cases, they forsake their families and old friends. They gradually adopt a life-style that demands dedication but protects them from temptation or anxiety. As Joel MacCollam states:

> A Christian is called by God to be a light in the world; the only way to be such a light is to be in the world but not of the world—to live among sinners without sharing sin.

The wooden goodness that most cultists adopt may more appropriately be a fragile veneer. Unlike the Christian Mac-Collam cites, cultists remain safely within the confines of the group, except when upon their missions. The cult wraps its communal cocoon about them, feeds them, clothes them, allays their misgivings, rewards their obedience, and in "protecting them from the world," nourishes them on platitudes at which the outside world might sneer. Certainly no one can claim that cultists lack devotion or discipline or perseverance or willingness to sacrifice. Yet it is far easier to seek perfection with people who are all following the same path toward the same goals. Seeking perfection becomes significantly harder, certainly a far greater test of the strength of one's beliefs, when one must live in an imperfect world.

CHAPTER NINE

GETTING OUT

Although the high turnover in cults seems to prove that cults are not nearly as effective at ensnaring recruits as is rumored and that people can and do leave on their own in great numbers, it may be that certain personalities are just more susceptible to coercive techniques than others. It is as likely that cult indoctrination techniques are effective only with some people, as it is that some people cannot be hypnotized. Many of those who join cults are too strong-willed to subject their needs and desires and thoughts to the will of someone else. Some "try on" cults as just another fad. Some, the less idealistic, don't really care about changing the world, and they eventually grow bored listening to cult platitudes. Some are even kicked out of cults. People do leave for any number of reasons, and the fact that they have voluntarily rejected the cult seems to disprove accusations of "mind control" or "brainwashing." Yet, if everyone could voluntarily reject cults, they would be of little concern.

But cults are of great concern. Despite the fact that many followers are able to leave on their own, others are not. If what Dr. John G. Clark, Jr., says is accurate, that this kind of thought process can't be reversed, the possibility exists that some cultists may never leave on their own. Certainly testimony from those who have been forcibly removed from the cults bears this out. "If my parents hadn't taken me out, I'd still be there," or "I could never have done it on my own," are statements heard time and again. Testimony of that sort cannot be disregarded. The radical personality change that so astonishes parents and old friends cannot be disregarded. Nor can the warnings of psychiatrists, psychologists, clergymen, and researchers who have no personal involvement with the cults or anything to gain from denouncing them.

The fact is that many parents have not seen their children in years. Some do not even know where they are or if, in fact, they are still alive. The longer a recruit remains with the cult, the greater his or her subservience to it and the less the chances are that the recruit will leave it. The effects that cult subservience has upon the mind may be so extreme that the cultist, even if forcibly removed, may not be able to function in society. He or she may find decision making overwhelming and run back to the cult for safety. One of Moon's followers whom Barbara Underwood cited in *Hostage to Heaven,* said to her, "I can't wait till we're slaves again."

Those who are incapable of getting out on their own must depend on others to do it for them. The responsibility most often is their parents'. Parents have a limited number of alternatives. They can wait, hoping the recruit will eventually grow bored. They can ask the recruit to come home for a week to talk. They can hire a lawyer and go to court to ask for custody or temporary conservatorship, or guardianship, of the recruit. Or they can call in a "deprogrammer," someone skilled in techniques which break down the cults' power over the mind and behavior of individual followers.

"Deprogramming" is a term originated by Ted Patrick, who is famous for the successful removal of hundreds of people from cults. It implies the undoing of programming or brainwashing. It is a new field, newer than brainwashing, and it is not foolproof. When it does not work and the cultist

returns to a cult, it can further alienate the follower from his or her family and the outside world.

Those for whom deprogramming has worked have great things to say about it. Many claim it is a thought-provoking, sensitive process in which all who participate grow. The cults claim it is violent, demeaning, and a threat to the dignity and freedom of anyone who participates. When Barbara Underwood's parents went to court to gain temporary custody of her, the cult gave Barbara a manual called *The Constructive Destruction of Religious Beliefs* published by an organization partly funded by the Church of Scientology. The Unification Church was preparing her for her deprogramming should it lose the court battle over her. She tells how terrorized she became:

> I was convinced the physical abuse it described did occur—the total humiliation, including forced nudity, sleeplessness, lack of food, even the forced defecation on pictures of cult leaders, and the possible use of rape and seduction.

The cults warn their followers that deprogramming is Satan himself trying to undermine their faith. They advise followers that they will be bombarded with trumped up "facts" and allowed no questions. Deprogramming will be the great test of their beliefs. To many recruits, so horrible is the specter of being kidnapped and deprogrammed that they grow increasingly distrustful of their parents, less desirous of seeing them, and further alienated from the outside world.

The deprogramming of any cultist is arranged well ahead of time. To the cultist, it is a "plot" formed and carried out against his will. He is "kidnapped" from the cult. Pehaps, as in

The well-known deprogrammer,
Ted Patrick

the case of Chris Edwards, a family member has come to take him out to dinner. In the case of Barbara Underwood, the court had decreed her removal. No matter how well meaning parents may be, initially, the cultist can only see his situation as that of a prisoner. Escape is uppermost in his mind. Deprogramming, then, is almost always off to a bad start. Resentment, hostility, fear, anger, and a sense of betrayal are all negatives that have to be overcome if the deprogramming is to be successful.

The cultists have been told not to talk, that conversing with "Satan" will allow "Satan" to get to them. They are advised to close their ears, not to listen, to shut "Satan" out. Often the cultists try to block themselves off from those around them with chanting or trances. They believe their new life is at stake.

The deprogrammer knows the recruits have been warned and trained to resist the outside world. He must somehow outwit the cultists. His ultimate goal is to restore the individual's thinking and decision-making capacities. He wants the cultist to make a decision against the cult. He believes that this will happen when the cultist clearly and thoroughly understands the motives of those who recruited him, the methods they used and their effect on the cultist's freedom and thinking abilities.

Deprogrammers are secretive about their methods. The more they make public the techniques they use, the more likely that recruits will be even better prepared to thwart them. The basic process is confrontation. The cultist believes the things he has been taught. The deprogrammer must present information that undermines those beliefs. The recruit spouts doctrine; the deprogrammer questions and probes until fallacies, holes in logic or reason or fact, are discovered. Often those holes in logic begin to appear with discussion of cult philosophy or doctrine. Ted Patrick asked Chris Edwards how many times he'd read Divine Principle or if he'd ever finished it. Edwards had to admit he hadn't. Patrick replied:

Do you know anybody in the cult who has read the whole thing? They don't give you time to read and think about it, because if you ever did, you'd see that it's all nonsense.

Patrick then went on to show Edwards passages that although taken from the Bible, were completely out of context. When compared to Moon's teachings, in context, they contradicted much of what he said.

Through questions and counter-questions, the deprogrammer hopes to show the cultist that he has been manipulated, and points out inconsistencies in what he has been taught. It is a difficult process, an extremely challenging process, and cannot be successful unless the deprogrammer is qualified. It should not be attempted by novices, no matter how well meaning.

When it is effective, deprogramming can reverse the effect of mind control. Deprogrammers make use of ex-cultists because they have inside information about the workings of the cults and often they know or have had a close relationship with the person being deprogrammed. Such was the case with Barbara Underwood. Two of her closest friends in the Unification Church who had already been deprogrammed assisted in Barbara's deprogramming.

The deprogramming process has several phases. The cult leader must be discredited. Doing so undermines the entire movement and the theology the recruit has adopted. In some cases, information to discredit the leader is readily obtainable. With other cults, that is not often so easy. Facts are necessary, not just vague insinuations. Testimony by ex-cultists, lawsuits, provable facts about the leader's behavior which contradict the very word he preaches, these are things with which a successful deprogrammer is armed. Often local pastors or psychiatrists who attempt to talk someone out of the cult, find themselves at a loss, even in this first stage, because they do not have enough ready facts when they are needed. A skillful deprogrammer has thoroughly studied the cult to which his subject belongs. Edwards remembers thinking that Patrick knew a lot more about the Divine Principle than he ever had.

The second phase requires the recruit's participation; the recruit must talk so that the deprogrammer can pinpoint areas of doubt. Perhaps the cultist secretly wonders just how "divinely inspired" the cult's leader really is. Perhaps he or she wonders where the money that is collected goes or what programs it supports, or wonders about the loss of his or her own ability to question, or whether cult life is really desirable after all. By listening, the deprogrammer can find vulnerable areas which he will then probe more deeply, looking for a way to crack the fortress the recruit has built around him and eventually a way to crumble its foundation.

A turning point occurs when the recruit willingly or unwillingly begins to listen. At this point, the process becomes less confrontational and more conversational, even if the cultist is still arguing his cause. Perhaps now the cultist will begin to question, begin to see connections, and begin to see that he has been manipulated.

When that happens, the final stage of "identification and transference" begins. The cultist sees he has been duped. The person who has accomplished this revelation is the deprogrammer. They two are on the same side. The cultist identifies with the deprogrammer. Together they become opponents of the cult.

According to Dr. John G. Clark, Jr., who was mentioned before, deprogramming should be called "repersonalization." He says the process restores the cultist's ability to make personal choices, to employ old language skills, and to bring back memories and old relationships. The process has given back the recruit's rightful personality, and the recruit is now in control again. As Barbara Underwood put it:

The hearing and deprogramming allowed me to be an individual, not a cultist, and in the act of looking at myself apart from the movement, I didn't like what I saw . . . It was . . . release from the womblike security of absolutes and guarantees, the perfect future universes that had blinded me.

Deprogramming is costly, but most parents who have tried other methods that failed are willing to spend the money to retrieve their children. Complete deprogramming cannot be done in just a few hours or days. Often rehabilitation takes weeks after the initial deprogramming. It is best done with the guidance of trained, highly qualified psychiatrists and medical staffs. Some provide several weeks of pertinent activities— courses in mind control, principles of the Bible, and family relationships. These centers enable the new ex-cultist time to relax, to think for him- or herself, to learn more about what happened, and to prepare for the difficulties ahead.

Those difficulties will be many. "Floaters," those who have recently left the cult, are in real danger of returning to the cult, floating back, for a long time after they make the decision to leave. The lost security of the cult is difficult to replace in the outside world, no matter how much love and affection parents shower upon them. They have been dissociated for some time from old friends, old groups, and old activities. During that time, they have had many experiences. Estrangement, uncertainty, constant memories, many of them good ones, guilt, feelings of having betrayed friends, any or all of these will be a part of their life for some time to come.

Decision making is especially hard for ex-cultists. If they really believe that they have been duped by the cult, they may be afraid of being again duped by someone else. They have little trust in their own perceptions. Having once been so wrong, they may think they lack the ability to perceive things accurately again. If they did something stupid once, they wonder if they are likely to do it again. Additionally, they are not used to making decisions. Like almost any other skill, decision-making becomes easier the more one does it and the more confident one is about it. Those skills are rusty. The floater is all too aware of how rusty. And that makes him tense.

Not only does his inner foundation seem shaky, but often the cult he has rejected will try to make contact with him to persuade him to come back. At this time he is not very strong and perhaps not all that sure he made the correct decision. Certainly he does not feel happy. The cult has a good chance of catching him at the right time with just the right kind of persuasion. Old friends within the cult may write letters and make phone calls either to reach the lost cultist or intimidate his or her family. Chris Edwards tells of a number of "suspicious" events that occurred the moment he left the cult. Although a female detective had been hired to guard his mother, two men still forcibly entered their home, breaking the chain latch and knocking the detective down. They left only when she drew her gun. Vans followed his family, his house was broken into twice, and the family's telephone was tampered with. The harassment was so frightening that Edwards's family hired live-in detectives for twenty-four hour protection. They continued to employ them for four months following his deprogramming.

Ex-cultists also experience a variety of illnesses. For some, lethargy, the inability to do anything, will make them too tired to cope. One individual, described by Stoner and Parke, spent nearly a year in bed before recovering. Others find their experiences so confusing that they think they might be going crazy. Others have great difficulty relating to people; they have no rules to follow and they are not sure what to expect from others. This is especially true in dating. Many ex-cultists left rigidly enforced environments with strict sexual practices, such as the chastity of the Unification Church or the celibacy of the Hare Krishnas. Now, released from those restrictions, the ex-cultists are truly befuddled, self-conscious, and uncertain.

So tenuous is the status of those recently deprogrammed that many actually do return to the cult. According to Stoner and Parke, every successful deprogramming case has a failed counterpart. Failure to successfully deprogram is disastrous, for the cultist returns to the cult with an even stronger faith and determination.

Possibly no attempt to reintegrate some cultists with society will ever work. If it is a structured, unquestioning, obedient, and rule-determined life that cultists want, they are going to find it somewhere or create it themselves. Perhaps they will never be at ease without that structure. Perhaps they will never be happy in situations that require independent decision-making and the ability to stand alone. In the final measure, it is up to the recruits. They have had a chance to see life from many perspectives. They are as informed as they will ever be. They have lived lost freedom in the cult, and have regained that freedom with the help of deprogrammers. Whether they choose to keep it, despite fear and uncertainty, is totally up to them.

CHAPTER
TEN

DRAWING
CONCLUSIONS

Are all religions good? The past two and one-half decades have shown that all religions are not good. Certainly those groups that masquerade as religions merely to get around laws or avoid taxes are not good. Those groups that use their followers as pawns to attain wealth or power are not good. Groups led by individuals whose motives and judgment are specious are not good. And if the accusations about brainwashing are, in fact, correct, religions that, for whatever reason, condone mind manipulation are not good. While some cults make no claim to being religious, others use religious status for the advantages it provides. Others, like the Unification Church, claim to be religious and have developed a complex philosophy that seems to justify a frightening number of nonreligious activities. And some cults began as religions but have moved away from God by creating new gods in the form of egomaniacs and unscrupulous messiahs.

Are all cults bad? It is impossible to answer that question without making sweeping generalizations as dangerous as believing all religions are good. Certainly religious freedom is good. Certainly the right to choose one's own religion is good.

The right to dedicate oneself to whatever degree one chooses is good. All of these freedoms are basic to American philosophy and the longevity of democracy. But when an individual or group preys upon unwitting citizens, using basic freedoms to operate with impunity, the law must find ways to protect its people.

Ted Patrick, speaking before the Dymally Committee of the California legislature said that freedom of religion, as defined in our constitution, is now antiquated. He calls it "a license to kill, lie, and steal" with impunity under the protection of church status.

Lying, stealing, and murder on the part of specific cults has been documented. Certainly Jim Jones murdered the children placed in his care when he decreed a mass "suicide" for his followers in Guyana. Those children were hardly capable of making wise decisions. Reported clubbings and beatings by Synanon members, not to mention the attempted murder for which three pled no contest, are on record. Spying and bugging of government offices on the part of Scientologists is also court record. Even Moon's "Heavenly Deception" justifies lying for the sake of the success of the Unification Church. There is no question that several cults or cult leaders have believed themselves above the law.

Alan Goldhammer, a constitutional lawyer, also speaking before the Dymally Committee, differentiated between the right to freedom of conscience and belief and the right to actually carry out those beliefs.

One may believe anything he chooses. That does not give him the right to break the law. This is the crux of the issue. In the case of the People vs. Collins, the defense argued that Collins had the right to use marijuana to "intensify religious belief and engage in religious experience." Marijuana, then, was part of the religious ritual. Collins lost because the government maintained that although Collins had every right to *believe* marijuana acceptable and useful in the practice of his religion, he had no right to use it (carry out his belief) when possession and use of the drug is illegal. Goldhammer continued:

If existing laws do not reach the problem and it is still felt that conduct is wrongful, assuming that a true religious belief is found and not a facade designed to conceal illegal activities, then legislation to prevent practices must be devised which will not interfere with the belief and which will demonstrate a compelling interest based on the protection of the health and safety of the public.

Goldhammer foresees designing laws for the protection and safety of the public when they become necessary. Those laws may be deterrents to cults now utilizing gray areas of the law for their own purposes. But designing such laws must be done with care. Solicitation laws designed to deter cults from fund raising within city limits might make it impossible for worthy groups to cut through the red tape and undermine their efforts. Zoning laws can and have been used by bigots against many traditional religions. Still, no legitimate group would be harmed by laws requiring clear disclosure of one's parent organization. Recruiting groups could no longer use lofty-sounding titles such as the Organization for Peace and Harmony without clearly stating that the group is an arm of a specific cult. People fund raising on street corners and door to door might be required to wear name tags exhibiting their parent organization's name so that the potential donor would know where his or her money was going before pulling out a wallet.

Yet laws designed to control cults may only be medications to treat symptoms, not the disease. They may deter cults, but they are not likely to stop them. Otherwise, how can the continued existence of a cult that advocates prostitution be explained? How can a cult that advocated bugging of government offices continue to attract members? Or a cult whose leader pled no contest to an attempted murder charge? Why do people continue to join cults that use aliases, or misrepresent their real mission? Is it simply ignorance of the facts or is it something else?

No documentation is available on the number of individuals who are recruited each year by cults, but unquestionably, that number is sizeable. Although the vast number of recruits are young people, everyone is a target of cult persuasion. The tentacles of cult influence reach into every segment of American society. Boundaries of religion, sex, age, income status, or even psychological stability simply do not exist. Cults extend their influence from lone individuals to government agencies. They effect the pocketbook of single citizens as well as national industries. The chance that one will know somebody who joins a cult or even be recruited oneself grows more likely. They do not just effect other people—they effect the society as a whole.

Are cults truly dangerous? Any organization or group that advocates blind obedience not only endangers the individual but freedom itself. When questioning is discouraged, let alone punished, personal as well as societal growth ceases. Humankind's greatest progress has always occurred at those times when individuals have been encouraged to question, to evaluate, and to create new answers. Anything that stymies that openness does so either because it cannot cope with change or it cannot withstand legitimate scrutiny. History has shown that leaders who fear questioning have been those who sensed they would lose if it were allowed.

Cults that advocate blind obedience ask their followers to give up the very gift that differentiates humankind from the rest of the animal world. That is the mind. With it, humanity has been able to move from mere savage beast to enlightened individual. Without it, individuality and free will cannot exist. If enough people betray that gift of the mind and free choice, anything can happen. Nazi Germany is horror in the extreme. But the bloated, decaying world of Jonestown and the ironic sign that greeted those who spent the next several weeks identifying bodies teaches the same lesson:

> Those who do not remember the past
> Are condemned to repeat it.

FOR
FURTHER
READING

This is not a complete list of the research materials used in the preparation of this book. Some of the books recommended by Free Minds, Inc. have also been added to this list.

Allen, Steve. *Beloved Son: A Story of the Jesus Cults.* Indianapolis: Bobbs-Merrill Co., 1982.

Boettcher, Robert, and Freedman, Gordon L. *Gifts of Deceit: Sun Myung Moon, Tongsun Park and the Korean Scandal.* New York: Holt, Rinehart and Winston, 1980.

Briggs, Dorothy C. *Your Child's Self-Esteem: The Key to His Life.* New York: Doubleday, 1970.

Bulgiosi, Vincent, and Gentry, C. *Helter Skelter.* New York: Norton, 1974.

Collier, Sophia. *Soul Rush.* New York: William Morrow, 1978.

Conway, Flo, and Siegelman, Jim. *Snapping.* New York: Delta, 1979.

Daner, Francine. *The American Children of Krishna: A Study of the Hare Krishna Movement.* New York: Holt, Rinehart and Winston, 1976.

Edwards, Christopher. *Crazy for God.* Englewood Cliffs, N.J.: Prentice-Hall, 1979.

Enroth, Ronald. *Youth, Brainwashing, and Extremist Cults.* Grand Rapids, MI: Zondervan (paperback), 1977.

_____ _The Lure of the Cults._ Chappaqua, N.Y.: Christian Herald Books, 1979.

Evans, Christopher. _Cults of Unreason._ New York: Farrar, Straus, and Giroux, 1974.

Hedley, James. _The Youth Nappers._ Wheaton, IL.: Victor Books.

Horowitz, Irving L. _Science, Sin, and Scholarship._ Cambridge, Mass: The MIT Press, 1978.

Judah, J. Stillson. _Hare Krishna and The Counterculture._ New York: John Wiley and Sons, 1974.

Kildruff, Marshall, and Javers, Ron. _The Suicide Cult._ New York: Bantam Books, 1978.

Krause, Charles A. _The Guyana Massacre._ New York: Berkley Publishing Corp., 1978.

Lifton, R. J. _Thought Reform and The Psychology of Totalism._ New York: Norton, 1961.

MacCollam, Joel. _Carnival of Souls._ New York: Seabury, 1979.

Marcuse, Frederick L. _Hypnotism: Fact and Fiction._ New York: Penguin, 1959.

Mills, Jeannie. _Six Years with God._ New York: A & W Publishers, 1979.

Mitchell, Dave and Cathy, Ofshe, Richard. _The Light on Synanon._ New York: Wideview Books, 1982.

Patrick, Ted, and Dullak, Tom. _Let Our Children Go!_ New York: E. P. Dutton, 1976.

Peterson, W. J. _These Curious New Cults._ New Canaan, Conn.: Keats, 1975.

Sargent, W. _Battle for the Mind._ New York: Harper & Row, 1971.

Sontag, Frederick. _Sun Myung Moon._ Nashville: Abingdon, 1977.

Stoner, Jo Anne and Parke, Carroll. _All God's Children._ Radnor, Pa.: Chilton, 1977.

Underwood, Barbara and Betty. _Hostage to Heaven._ New York: Clarkson and Potter, 1979.

Wooden, Kenneth. _The Children of Jonestown._ New York: McGraw-Hill, 1981.

INDEX